PARENTING: THE RULES

THE ALWAYS | THE NEVERS

*20 transformational precepts to
change the children of the world
in one generation*

BY SUSAN M. THOMSON, PHD

Books may be ordered through booksellers or by contacting:

Wainwright Global
www.WainwrightGlobal.com
1 (800) 711-4346

Because of the dynamic nature of the Internet, any web addresses or links contained in this book may have changed since publication and may no longer be valid. The views expressed in this work are solely those of the authors and do not necessarily reflect the views of the publisher, and the publisher hereby disclaims any responsibility for them.

The authors of this book do not dispense medical advice or prescribe the use of any technique as a form of treatment for physical, emotional, or medical problems without the advice of a physician, either directly or indirectly. The intent of the author is only to offer information of a general nature to help you in your quest for becoming a better parent. In the event you use any of the information in this book for yourself, which is your constitutional right, the author and the publisher assume no responsibility for your actions.

Photographer credits – Eric Quiros
Illustrator credits – Reigel Allen Munsayac
Cover design - Reigel Allen Munsayac
Publisher – Wainwright Global, Inc.

ISBN: 979-8-9912217-4-0 (sc)
ISBN: 979-8-9912217-3-3 (hc)
ISBN: 979-8-9912217-5-7 (e)

Library of Congress Pre-Assigned Control Number: 1-14989851241
Library of Congress Registration Number: TXu 2-517-478

Wainwright Global rev. date: 01/09/2026

Table of Contents

Parenting: The Rules

~ The Nevers ~

~ The Always ~

~ Notes ~

Dedication

I dedicate this book to my son, Demian, who was raised according to these Twenty Rules. Some of the rules were known from the start; others were discovered along the way.

Demian has grown into a person of great generosity, humanity, and kindness. He has a wide circle of friends who admire and care for him. His wife, Rachel, once shared that one of her favorite things about Demian is that it seems everyone around him loves him. This is true! He is deeply intuitive and demonstrates a high level of emotional intelligence.

When Demian was a young child, several friends and relatives believed we were "spoiling" him by refusing to use conventional parenting techniques such as punishment, the withdrawal of privileges, grounding, or—even more concerning—spanking. We were proud that, through regular and meaningful conversations about feelings, we never had to resort to those methods—nor would we have. That ongoing dialogue made it easier to avoid all of the "Nevers" outlined in this book.

Anyone who knows Demian would agree that he is an extraordinary person. He is intelligent, handsome, athletic, fit, highly social, and fun. I truly believe that when parents raise their children using these Twenty Rules, they too will one day describe their adult children with the same pride and joy with which I describe my son, Demian.

By using these Twenty Rules of parenting, we have the power to change the world in just one generation.

Foreword

As a retired U.S. Army Chaplain with 24 years of service, I have witnessed firsthand the profound effects that military deployment can have on children across all developmental stages—from infants and toddlers to school-age children and teenagers. The emotional challenges these families face, particularly the stress of separation from loved ones, highlight just how critical effective parenting strategies become during times of family disruption. Research consistently demonstrates that strong parenting practices serve as essential buffers against deployment-related stressors and significantly aid in children's adjustment and resilience.

It is within this context of understanding family stress and child development that Dr. Susan M. Thomson's Parenting: The Rules emerges as particularly valuable. Having counseled countless military families through the challenges of deployment cycles, I recognize the urgent need for parenting approaches that prioritize emotional connection and psychological safety.

Parenting in the 21st century presents unprecedented challenges. In an era of information overload and rapidly changing cultural norms, many parents search for guidance that feels both principled and practical. Dr. Thomson's work challenges traditional authoritarian parenting methods, from physical punishment to emotional manipulation. Her twenty rules invite readers to examine not only their techniques but also the underlying beliefs that drive them.

The military and civilian environments often emphasize discipline, structure, and compliance—values that, while important in certain contexts, can sometimes overshadow the equally crucial need for emotional attunement and responsive caregiving. Dr. Thomson's approach emphasizes emotional intelligence, choice-giving, abundant provision, and unconditional positive regard—principles I have seen transform struggling families.

What distinguishes this work is its unflinching critique of practices many consider necessary. Dr. Thomson argues against time-outs, chores, forced sharing, and grounding—positions that may seem counterintuitive to parents concerned about raising responsible children. Her alternative approach, grounded in attachment theory and developmental psychology, offers practical solutions that strengthen rather than strain parent–child relationships.

The book's strength lies in integrating research-based insights with practical applications. From explaining biblical references about "sparing the rod" to discussing the psychological effects of praise, Dr. Thomson bridges academic knowledge and everyday parenting decisions. Her exploration of developmental stages provides helpful context for understanding children's changing needs.

This book offers a valuable perspective on child development. The author's passion for protecting children is both evident and admirable, and parents are encouraged to adapt these insights in ways that best fit their family's needs and values.

This work will resonate most with parents seeking alternatives grounded in psychological research and genuine care for children's emotional development. For military families navigating the unique stresses of service life, and for all parents seeking to raise resilient, emotionally healthy children, *Parenting: The Rules* offers validation and practical guidance for a more compassionate approach to raising the next generation.

Juan Loya, PhD, MDiv
U.S. Army Chaplain, Colonel, Retired
Board-Certified Chaplain and Clinical Pastoral Counselor/Educator

Introduction

Parenting is a daunting job. Most people say that no one has provided them any real training or even a manual on how to be successful in this endeavor. As many parents often say, "No one ever gave me a rule book on how to be successful in the job of parenting." Others wonder why we do not have parenting classes in high school that show us how to fundamentally navigate our most important job in the world. We learned higher math like geometry or calculus, which has its merits, yet we do not learn the most basic key rules for effective parenting.

If each of us could have the knowledge to successfully parent, we could change the world in one generation. I believe that this is a very important goal and actually doable. We need to be well educated in what works and what doesn't. We also need to understand ourselves to a certain degree in order to be a good parent. If we can be kind to and effectively discipline ourselves, we can be kind to and effectively discipline our children.

I use the word discipline loosely. What I generally mean by this is that we intentionally and with full awareness make good decisions about ourselves and our children. I see discipline more as an idea that allows us to carefully think through what our desires and goals are, rather than just letting things happen. When we have discipline in our lives, events happen in a more intentional way because we have thought about and planned for them ahead of time.

This is what we need to do as parents. We need to think about what we want for ourselves and for our children. Happiness? Success? Joy? High self-esteem? Functional relationships? All of the above?

Most people will espouse wanting their children to become happy, good citizens and create prosperity in their adult lives. Of course, there are many notions about good parenting. But most fathers and mothers unconsciously—and often mindlessly—repeat how they were parented, even if they despised and resented it at the time. You may even hear yourself saying, "I'm not going to do that to my child when I'm a parent," and then find yourself doing that exact thing.

For example, as a young child, you may have been repeatedly left alone at home and told to do your chores, and then find yourself years later doing that same thing to your son or daughter, all the while justifying your behavior. Once becoming a parent, it can be difficult to even see that you are repeating "the sins of the father onto the children."

Without self-knowledge, awareness, and an understanding of the important aspects of parenting, we are essentially destined to repeat the past. It is a psychological phenomenon that if we are in denial about our past, we repeat it as a way of suppressing the pain that we do not want to feel, in tandem with defending our parents from their responsibility and culpability. We do not do this with ignorance or malice. We do it because we cannot deal effectively with the truth of our own childhoods.

The central core of "bad parenting" is not acknowledging the needs and feelings of the child. When a child is angry, we put him or her in "time out" or tell them that being angry is bad and that their anger should not be expressed, rather than listening and understanding how they feel.

When a young boy falls down and cries because he skinned his knee, we tell him to "be a man and stop crying," or "it wasn't all that bad."

If a young girl becomes angry with her younger siblings, she is told to be "nice," because he is younger than she.

As we deny the child's thoughts and feelings and tell them that what they are feeling is wrong or silly or cowardly, we set the stage for repression and the ensuing repetition compulsion—the unwitting passing on of destructive and ineffective parenting.

This is the passageway by which destructive parenting is passed down generation to generation. Another very potent and destructive part of the psychology of repetition compulsion lies in defending the dysfunctional parenting we received.

I have heard comments like, "My father whipped me with a belt, but I turned out all right. It must not have been that bad." This, of course, is a rationale to pass on this painful and ineffective parenting technique. Once certain dysfunctional ideas have set into families, we can refer to this as a "generational curse."

This is the belief that it's always been done this way, so it must be genetic or at least the right thing to do. It feels inescapable.

I say to you, there is an escape from the generational dysfunction of poor parenting and the resulting unhappy childhoods passed down from parent to child. As has been said in jest or sarcasm, "It's never too late to have a happy childhood."

I've found that there are 20 essential rules for good parenting. When followed with clarity, consistency, and understanding of their intention, their implementation can make for happy children, emotionally intimate families, and effective parenting.

In these 20 rules, one might think I am somewhat simplifying the very tough, yet very rewarding, job of parenting. However, these ideas will create a solid foundation from which to parent with unconditional love, not the very harmful conditional love. With these guidelines, and an overall understanding of why these rules are so important, one can feel confident that he or she is on the right track to become a loving and effective mother or father.

These 20 rules may initially seem fantastical to some—and to others, even wrong. I challenge each reader to look deep into their own hearts and ask themselves if they would have liked to have been parented with these rules.

Would you have liked your parents to listen to you and to help you understand your feelings and how to effectively express them?

Would you have preferred your parents not call you names such as lazy or stupid?

Would you have preferred a discussion about why you feel so angry at your mother or father, rather than being sent to your room until you didn't feel that way any longer, and then have to come out and apologize for something that you don't feel sorry for?

We all have hurts from our past. No parent is perfect. And all parents can be overwhelmed with the essential nature of providing for and having children.

One "get out of jail free card" for making mistakes as a parent is as follows—apologize!

It is imperative to know that we will not, by definition of being human, be perfect parents. Yet we all have the ability to apologize to our children for any transgression we may commit.

We may yell at the top of our lungs at the child who is late for an important appointment. As unnecessary and often absurd as this can be, we do these things.

We can absolve ourselves from the guilt of having done these things to our children that we later regret. We just need to tell them we are sorry and that parents do make mistakes.

An admission of wrongdoing from a parent to a child creates emotional intimacy and safety for children.

Feeling safe in the family environment—where feelings are explored and expressed by both parents and children—helps create the happy family we're looking for.

https://parentingtherules.com

PARENTING: THE RULES

THE ALWAYS | THE NEVERS

20 transformational precepts to change the children of the world in one generation

BY SUSAN M. THOMSON, PHD

THE NEVERS

PARENTING | THE RULES

Use these eleven rules with care and wisdom

to shape a better future for your children

Chapter 1

Never Strike, Spank or Yell at Your Child

Traditionally, spanking children has been part of American culture and has been seen as a way for parents to feel they are "disciplining" their children properly. These parents hold the false belief that they are teaching obedience and respect for authority, and that this is necessary to form a well-behaved child—and, subsequently, a functioning adult who becomes a law-abiding citizen.

I believe most parents don't feel good about striking, hitting, or spanking their children, but often feel they have no alternative. Almost everyone is familiar with the biblical phrase "spare the rod, and spoil the child." Unfortunately, this paraphrased version of a verse in Proverbs has likely caused more pain and suffering for children than nearly any other reference of any kind.

In his article "The Truth About 'Spare the Rod and Spoil the Child,'" Nirvana Reginald Gayle writes that "the 'rod' is not the rod of a stick to beat your child with. It is the rod as in 'thy rod and thy staff comfort me,'" a quote from the 23rd Psalm. Throughout the Bible, many references are made to a rod or staff. For instance, in the biblical story of Moses, he carries a rod and parts the Red Sea to save the Hebrew people from annihilation. The Biblical rod is actually a symbol of righteous power, leadership, spiritual enlightenment and knowledge that goes beyond normal understanding. It can be seen as emblematic of guidance and wisdom, not of corporal punishment, violence, or physical abuse.

Shepherds did not carry rods or staffs to beat their sheep; they used them to guide and protect them, keeping the flock on the right path and safe from danger. The staff could be used to steer a sheep "who has gone astray" back into the fold, help navigate rough terrain or to defend the flock from predators. We need to adopt this same "shepherd" approach with our children—guiding and safeguarding them from danger with care and compassion.

I cite this biblical reference only because it has been so pervasive in American culture. Nirvana Reginald Gayle worked in child protective services in Los Angeles County for over 25 years. He believes that people often "beat their children in order to control them and get them to do what they want by justifying it with the 'spare the rod' Biblical reference." He also notes that adults who were beaten as children frequently use the rationale "I turned out all right" as a secondary excuse for continuing the cycle of beating their own children.

I am fairly certain that many parents are aware that this way of dealing with their children is not a positive one. However, I speak here to those parents who may still misunderstand what the Bible is truly trying to teach.

It is clear that the Bible is not trying to impart that hitting your children with a "rod" is a permissible or helpful method of parenting. In fact, it is a complete misunderstanding of what the Bible is trying to teach.

Indeed, our truest job as parents is to give our children the knowledge they need to live prosperous and happy lives. These ideas can only be transferred effectively through modeling, consistent communication, and the deliberate sound teaching of truth, honesty, and unconditional love.

In addition, when spanking or beating has been passed down generationally, children have little or no chance of escaping this cycle of corporal punishment. I recall my own father using his belt on my brother for perceived infractions. My sense is that he did not feel good about it but believed—perhaps as a devoted Catholic—that he must not "spare the rod.". In fact, he falsely believed it was his parental duty not to "spare the rod." He felt he needed to get my brother "in line" and that the belt was the most direct and effective method. I'm sure my brother would beg to differ.

The sad truth is that corporal punishment of children creates anger and resentment toward the offending parent. The child is likely to feel shame and experience lower self-esteem—but is unlikely to reduce or stop the targeted behavior at all. As has been well established in Skinnerian behavioral psychology, punishment only suppresses the behavior in the presence of the punisher. If you punish me for a behavior, I may avoid doing it in front of you—but I will likely continue it when you're not present. In other words, punishment does not eliminate behavior; it only drives it underground. So, in effect, the behavior is still in the child's repertoire and will most likely be performed outside the knowledge of the parent. It is highly likely that this is not the outcome most parents are hoping for.

Punishment as a parenting tool simply does not work. Parents are not meting out punishment just to do so out of retaliation or vengeance all the while knowing or believing it doesn't work. The parent is simply trying to rid the child of the offending behavior. However, many people have never heard nor do they understand that this is the outcome of punishment.

Another complication is the unconscious desire many of us have to protect our own parents from accountability for what they did to us. This is likely why some parents continue to employ techniques that go against their primal urge to protect their children from harm. In essence, parents repeat 'the sins of the father' and deliver them down to the children. The logic becomes circular: "I turned out okay" or "I deserved the beatings" or "My parents said it was for my own good and I believe them and still do." This denial helps perpetuate the cycle of intergenerational abuse.

A further danger of corporal punishment is that it can escalate. It can lead to even further physical or possibly sexual abuse. Where is the line between a swat on the bottom and more serious physical or sexual abuse? Repeated swatting of a child's bottom can become a sexual stimulus for some individuals so inclined. More broadly, acts of physical domination over children may generate a disturbing sense of control or power that instills fear in the child. Innocent-seeming spankings can become a gateway to deeply inappropriate behaviors. We must acknowledge that violence—physical, emotional, or sexual—is child abuse and should be viewed as such. We do not want to parent by fear or violence and usually only do so from a lack of appropriate parenting skills and the incorrect belief that our own abuse was somehow good for us.

Clearly, the best approach is to avoid physical punishment altogether. Most parents want to do right by their children. The problem is it can simply be a lack of parenting tools. Physical punishment can seem effective in the moment— but its long-term consequences are deeply damaging. In other words, parents resort to less than desirable behaviors when they don't know what else to do and the effect of implementing physical punishment is usually immediate and, therefore, can seem effective and satisfying

The irony is that punitive parenting using corporal punishment actually generates the violence and fear it is trying to prevent. Fear is the opposite of love. You cannot raise a healthy, secure child through fear. You cannot build trust, love and understanding through physical abuse. So, what can parents do instead of striking or hitting their children to help them understand how the world works and why their behavior may not be acceptable.

We begin by realizing that **communication** is the key. We must take time to talk to our children, helping them understand the reasons behind why we need them to behave in a particular fashion. Even small children can understand a compassionate and communicative parent.

According to Erik Erikson's theory of psychosocial development, two-year-olds are in the stage of seeking **autonomy** versus **shame and doubt**. They are asserting their independence and competence, their separateness and self-reliance. Parents who do not understand this natural phase may become frustrated and resort to force (spanking) to rein in their two-year-old because it appears that somehow the toddler who was previously compliant has become impossibly defiant. We even call it the "Terrible Two's." But autonomy is necessary for healthy psychological development. Success in this stage builds self-esteem; failure can lead to insecurity and shame.

Parents can support autonomy by offering limited choices: "Do you want to wear this outfit or that one?" or "Which toy would you like to bring in the car?" These small choices help toddlers feel a sense of control and reduce conflict. Of course, not all choices are safe—if a toddler tries to leap off a four-foot wall or climb the stairs backwards, we intervene with calm explanation, redirection, or assistance, not punishment. These behaviors are natural instincts of a young boy or girl trying out their physical skills and are not defiance or "bad" behavior.

My older brother who was the recipient of the "belt" in my family was whipped one day because at four years old he walked, alone and at a significant and dangerous distance from home, down to the local elementary school searching for my mother who was working there at the Catholic school fair. He was dressed in a white linen suit, white coat with white short pants, and white shoes. He had planned on going!! Today, my brother explains that my father "forgot" to take him so he took matters into his own hands. His self-determination and will got him there.

A subsequent beating with the belt was frankly unconscionable when an explanation of the danger of what he had done would have been adequate.

When I was growing up, the belief in physical punishment for "bad behavior" was held deeply in the collective unconscious. The **collective unconscious** is a concept introduced by Carl Jung which refers to a part of the human psyche that is inherited and shared by all humans. I use the term here more loosely to refer to long-held inappropriate or false beliefs that everyone seems to be in agreement about. The collective unconscious I am referring to influences our thoughts, our feelings and our behaviors and is often manifest in religion and ritual. This occurs without any conscious awareness. Our cultural agreement that corporal punishment is "normal" is one such belief. But society is changing, and we are waking up.

A parent who tries to impose their will on a young toddler child especially through corporal punishment will eventually create a child full of doubt, anxiety, frustration, and eventually rage. This stage is often characterized by mutual refusals—toddlers say "no," and parents say "no" back. But not every situation requires this kind of interaction. However, there are circumstances when "no" is the only answer (a hot stove)!

For example, if a child bangs pots and pans while the parent is on the phone, instead of yelling or hitting, the parent can say, "Thank you for not banging while I'm on the phone. I can't hear. You can choose a quiet toy. Which one do you want?" If that fails, redirecting the child physically or removing the pots and pans are also options. Admittedly, these approaches are more work than striking a child—but the long-term gain of a happy child is invaluable.

Yelling, like hitting, is abuse. It is the verbal abuse equivalent of Rule number one's physical abuse. The primary goal of each of these abuses is to instill fear in the child in order to get the child to obey or knuckle under to the parent and gain compliance. There is probably a large percentage of parents who use this technique in an attempt to "discipline" their children. But yelling, especially at a young child, is never appropriate. Children cannot understand context. They cannot understand that their parents may have problems. There is only one way for a young child to interpret a parents' yelling - it is totally their fault. They don't know the parent had a bad day at work or is worried about a sick loved one. All they know is that they are being yelled at—so they must be bad.

This leads to anxiety and toxic shame. In this home environment where yelling is constant and common, children learn to "walk on eggshells" around the offending parent or parents. They begin to see themselves as "fatally flawed" because no matter the situation, the parent is ultimately going to be yelling at them for some perceived bad behavior and they are virtually helpless to do anything about it.

When children are victims of any kind of abuse, they are fundamentally being abandoned by their parent. Abandonment sets up a feeling of shame, a feeling of being basically wrong or flawed in some innate way that they cannot escape or understand. In emotional abandonment, a child can only perceive that it is their own behavior that is the cause of their parents' unhappiness and subsequent abuse of them. The child may think that if they could figure out what they could do right, maybe they could stop this kind of abuse, in this case yelling. Abuse of any kind is a form of **abandonment**, and abandonment creates toxic shame.

Children make mistakes in order to learn. Children by their very nature are going to experiment, take risks and do things they probably shouldn't. A child cannot learn to walk without falling. Do we spank them or yell at them when they fall? No! We may rush to assist them to get back up and try again. We encourage them to keep trying and smile at their successes and ignore their failures. We stand a few feet away and beckon them toward us. We cheer loudly over the smallest accomplishment. Most parents innately behave this way and accept and understand how to do this. We must recognize that all parents have the correct parenting repertoire in them exhibited by how they treat their toddler who is learning to walk. But, when it comes to a multitude of other behaviors, often parents do not give their children the same latitude and understanding necessary for growth.

When an older child is learning to ride a bike, we begin with training wheels. We hold the back of the bike for support and rush to their assistance and comfort them if they fall and skin a knee. We give them plenty of time to learn this skill as it is an important passage of childhood to learn to ride a bike and most parents have a full understanding of this. Parents do not whip their child with a belt when they fall off a bike or yell at them for not learning quickly enough. We are patient, kind and generally we fully comprehend that it takes a certain amount of time to learn the skill of riding a bike. Happily, once learned, it is forever!

Here we have two clear examples of how appropriate parenting is implemented. The key elements include patience, understanding, encouragement, positive verbal feedback, comfort when failure occurs and cheering for the smallest of victories.

I say emphatically that all parents have this ability in their DNA if you will. We observe this kind of parenting on TV and movies and see it active in our own lives. Most, if not all, children are not punished for falling when learning to walk or yelled at when learning to ride a bike. So why do we not extend this same patience and compassion to other kinds of childhood learning? It basically makes no sense.

In any situation, we can use these same skills we inherently already know. One must come from the basic premise that children are good and want to be happy and please themselves and their parents. We must view our children as gifts from God that we have been so blessed to be able to create. I stand against any belief that says that infants are born with an inherent flaw or fault that must be removed through severe discipline or punishment. There is no innately bad characteristic of any newborn infant.

I must reemphasize that children want to be happy, to please themselves and their parents. They are not born flawed. The idea that children are inherently bad and need to be corrected through punishment is both false and harmful.

Psychological theory says that there are **temperament** differences at birth. Some children are easier, some more difficult, especially those affected by conditions like fetal alcohol syndrome or chronic colic. But temperament is not destiny. Current studies indicate that temperament is biologically rooted but can be changed through nurturing caregiving and a supportive environment. With the right care and set of loving circumstances, all children can thrive. Good parenting enhances a child's ability to succeed regardless of how they may have started in life.

The message is this: No baby is inherently bad. All children are inherently good. And all parents inherently already know how to nurture and compassionately parent their children. We do it instinctively when they learn how to walk. We just need to apply what we already know to any and all parenting situations that may arise.

Chapter 2

Never Lecture Your Child

For this rule, one needs only to remember being lectured when young. Ask yourself, "How much did I like being lectured for ten or fifteen minutes on topics of little interest, especially as a teenager?"

Lecturing on the virtue of building character, avoiding procrastination, or any similar topic where a parent drones on uninterrupted is sure to create a wall between parent and child. Modeling the behaviors you want your teenager to adopt is a far more effective tool to teach what you want your children to learn. For instance, if you want your child to learn not to "put off until tomorrow what can be done today," model that behavior.

A second technique is to simply share your own experiences. Engage your child in the conversation. Let's say it's Saturday and you need to wash the car. Instead of putting it off, you tell your teenage son or daughter that you're going to wash the car today so you can relax on Sunday. You might ask your child whether they've noticed it's better to get homework done sooner rather than later. In other words, discussing important life lessons through dialogue creates a loving and bonding experience. It's during the teen years that lecturing is most commonly used in an attempt to change or control behavior—yet it is mostly, if not entirely, ineffective.

However, it does have an effect: it fosters deep resentment toward the lecturing parent, even as the child tries to block out what is being said.

The most deleterious consequence of lecturing is that it lowers your child's self-esteem. If your child is struggling to complete a task, there is usually an emotional reason behind the behavior. It is more effective to explore that emotional reason that is controlling your child's behavior and preventing their success.

For example, if your child begins to fail in a particular subject, you may become alarmed and switch into lecture mode, warning about how poor grades might impact college admissions. You ask, "Don't you want to succeed in life?" or "Can't you just put in more time and realize that your study habits are not working for you?" These questions apply pressure and may shame the child, rather than uncover the root cause. Such exchanges create a barrier of resentment that separates you from your child. My guess is that this is not the goal of these questions. However, it is the result. Let's look at a better way.

A better approach might be: "How do you feel about your recent test scores?" or "Is there anything I can do to help?" or "Has something happened in class or elsewhere that might explain the change from B's to D's?" Perhaps your child needs a tutor. Maybe they're distracted by a new romantic relationship. It could even be that a teacher has become verbally abusive. There are countless possible reasons. But moralizing and condescending questions will not lead to honest answers or meaningful change.

One caveat is that if you've been a parent who tends to shame or lecture, your child might not initially know how to respond to your more empathic, solution-oriented questions. It may take time and several conversations to earn their trust. Your child may fear a return to the normal shaming. Give them time and reassurance that you genuinely care about their feelings.

It's also helpful to be transparent. Explain that you've realized lecturing has not been effective and that you want to try a better way. Now you really want to know what is truly going on and find out what their feelings are regarding the poor math grades and that you want to help your child solve the problem. You might say your own parents lectured you and that you endured it silently, though it was painful and unhelpful. Let your child know they're free to remind you if you start slipping back into lecturing. Old habits die hard, and you may not always notice when you're doing it again. Your child can be your best teacher—if you let them.

More important than solving any individual problem is the greater goal of helping your child explore and understand their own feelings. That's how people come to know who they are. Children need to learn that feelings are essential guides to identity and authenticity. A strong sense of one's own emotions leads to success in all areas of life, especially in intimate relationships. If a person is attuned to their own emotions, they'll be better able to understand and respect those of their future partner.

Getting in touch with one's feelings and then treating them with understanding and compassion builds self-esteem. When a child knows it's okay to feel hurt, sad, angry, or afraid—and that all people experience these emotions—they begin to accept and trust themselves. It is not unusual for a boy to feel hurt or a girl to feel angry.

If you lecture your child about poor grades, or any topic at all, they will likely feel that you don't value their perspective or care about their feelings. They may believe you care only about getting them to complete the task and then move on to the next demand.

This principle also applies when lecturing about serious issues like drugs or alcohol. If you're warning your child about substance abuse while abusing opioids yourself, the contradiction is glaring. Your message will be dismissed as hypocrisy and trust diminishes.

Understand that lecturing is a form of punishment meant to change behavior—but punishment only suppresses behavior temporarily and only in the presence of the punisher. It doesn't foster lasting change.

In Walter Isaacson's biography of Elon Musk, he writes about how Elon's father, Errol, would lecture him for hours during childhood. Elon's brother, Kimbal, described their father as "one minute he would be friendly, and the next he would be screaming at you, lecturing you for hours—literally two or three hours while he forced you to just stand there—calling you worthless, pathetic, making scarring and evil comments, not allowing you to leave." These sessions had a deeply damaging impact on Elon and severely strained their relationship. At seventeen, Elon "realized he would have to escape" and so he left South Africa for Canada, alone, two weeks before his eighteenth birthday.

A client of mine, an only child, was subjected to constant lectures by his father, even into later adulthood. During phone calls, his father would barrage him with a litany of probing questions about his business dealings and his daily life. In the beginning, the client could not really stop this line of questioning and endured the lecturing until he realized through our discussions how destructive and demeaning it truly was. Once my client believed that he did not deserve this type of treatment, he could more easily redirect the conversation away from these accusatory statements and, if necessary, end the phone call.

We used to call it "being bawled out," and it was common across families. But it served no constructive purpose. Tragically, some parents still use this approach with impunity and without remorse. Lecturing is an abusive parenting technique that fails to change behavior and leaves lasting scars on a child's self-worth.

Across all families, it needs to end.

Chapter 3

Never Put Your Child in "Time Out"

Time-out is overrated. However, it is preferable to spanking or yelling. Still, it is not ideal in effective parenting.

If a child is throwing a tantrum, putting them in time-out means you are leaving him or her alone without explanation and essentially abandoning the child during their most painful moments. If a child is throwing a tantrum because they are tired and hungry, how can a time-out fix this problem? For a child with trauma or attachment issues, this only exacerbates those issues.

Generally, a child repeatedly throws tantrums because they have been systematically rewarded by the parent into believing that this is the most effective way to get what they want. It can also occur because the child is overstressed due to lack of sleep, food, or attention. Additionally, it may happen because the child has little or no communication skills to express what they want.

I refer to tantrums as the primary example in this discussion, as I see no other remotely logical reason for putting a child in time-out. One might say that if two children get into an altercation and, for example, Johnny bites Joey, time-out for Johnny is necessary and well-deserved. Yet, there is a better way.

First, any and all medical needs should be addressed. Second, Joey needs to tell Johnny how much it hurt and how mad he is that Johnny bit him. Then, Johnny can say how he feels. He may say that he is mad because Joey broke his toy. Joey can say he didn't mean to—it was an accident. In this scenario, young children are learning to communicate effectively and appropriately in real time. They are explaining how the biting incident came about and expressing their feelings. The parent or teacher should remind Johnny, as Joey listens, "We don't bite at home/school. We use our words." Time-out in no way accomplishes the extraordinary experience these two children are having—problem-solving, sharing feelings, and understanding limit setting (no biting, only words).

Time-out for a tantrum is probably more effective for the parent, who may need to de-escalate rising feelings of anger and frustration. A time-out for a parent is always welcome as a primary tool to handle any difficult situation and can be very effective. Unfortunately, the same does not apply to the child.

A parent may be systematically reinforcing tantrum behavior and be completely unaware they are increasing, not decreasing, the unwanted behavior. This happens when the needs of the child are ignored. Before long, the child throws a tantrum. Parents must develop an awareness of the signals children give about what they want and need. If not, when children are placed in situations beyond their ability to cope meaningfully, a tantrum may ensue. If parents continually ignore their child's needs after one, two, or three requests, tantrums are likely to follow. If this becomes standard parenting behavior repeated across many different situations, children will "up the ante" for their parents' attention and ultimately use the tantrum to get a response—even if it's negative. Remember, negative attention can be preferable to no attention at all.

For example, a child in group play may be laughed at by others while the preoccupied parent ignores it. The child comes to the parent, who replies, "They are not laughing at you now, so go back and play." The child's desire for protection and sympathy has been denied. If this happens repeatedly, the child may "melt down" as the only way to fully elicit a protective response from the parent. If a child must get louder and louder to get a desired response, the parent is actually creating and reinforcing subsequent tantrum behavior.

Once, I went to the zoo with my sister-in-law and her young son. Upon entering, he immediately saw a stuffed animal (a snake) and wanted it badly. My sister-in-law told him there were many other stores in the zoo and that he should wait and look at all of them. Sounds reasonable, of course, if you are an adult. However, the young boy insisted this was what he wanted. I turned to her and said "The boy wants the snake." However, she ignored his request, and we went through the entire San Diego Zoo with him continually complaining and asking about the snake. After a full day of this, he finally got his snake and happily wrapped it around his neck as we left (it was the best toy in the park). No tantrum occurred, but it certainly could have. The situation was completely unnecessary, as the boy's zoo experience—and ours—was overshadowed by his upset.

Solutions, you say? Yes, and a very easy one. The mother, of course, was worried that he would see other toys and want those as well, and she only wanted to purchase one.

I insert here that the vast majority of parenting solutions reside in communication with your child. In this case, the mother could have told her child that yes, he could have the snake, but it would be his only toy choice of the day. He could choose the snake now or look around and choose later. I am certain he would have chosen the snake at the beginning of the day and been perfectly content the rest of the time.

We must trust our children to know what they want and help them learn the boundaries around receiving it. Here, the boundary was that there would be only one toy. He could make the choice at any time.

In this scenario, the young boy could have accomplished two things. He could make his choice and feel empowered by getting what he wanted. He could also learn that his choice had a limit—there was only one. Children can accept real, day-to-day limitations and boundaries if they are explained ahead of time and if you trust them. Children are amazingly intuitive and brilliant beings who, when given the chance, can succeed in making good choices and can understand the consequences placed before them.

Suffice it to say, had her son thrown a tantrum over the snake, there was no time-out room at the zoo. You can't carry a time-out room with you throughout your child's life. Better to let go of the idea that this is a reasonable or effective parenting tool. In fact, studies show that 85 percent of parents use time-out incorrectly (too long or too punitively) and that it can actually increase misbehavior.

In adult recovery programs, the HALT acronym is taught as a way to identify situations that may tempt an addict to use—when they are Hungry, Angry, Lonely, or Tired. Psychiatrist and author Dr. Dan Siegel also uses a child-focused version called HALTSS: Hungry, Angry, Lonely, Tired, Stressed, and Sick. If parents focus on these unmet needs as the root causes of tantrums, their children won't have to resort to such behavior because the parent will address the needs long before the tantrum occurs.

It is disconcerting to realize that society focuses on the child as misbehaving when they throw a tantrum, rather than on the true cause: the parent is misbehaving. The parent is not carefully observing the child's unmet needs or understanding the "pre-tantrum signals" the child is giving. A very young child who is hungry, tired, and maybe even ill—and who cannot express their needs—may only have the tantrum to fall back on if the parent lacks appropriate awareness. If this lack of awareness spans many situations, the tantrum behavior will worsen.

Let me repeat: the primary reason for tantrums in children is that they are repeatedly put into frustrating, anger-producing situations where they cannot understand the decisions being made around them. They then must increase their negative behavior to get what they want, and when further frustrated, a tantrum occurs. For instance, a child may not even know they are hungry or tired. It is the duty of the parent to be aware of the child's needs.

It is also the parent's duty to communicate with their child and explain the limits and boundaries of life. Parents must give children reasonable choices so they feel empowered and understand the consequences of their choices.

Children need to have an appropriate amount of power over their own lives. They need to be able to choose the stuffed animal at the zoo. Choice is key to giving children the experience of understanding the consequences of their behavior. There is no better way to teach this. Life is about making choices, succeeding, and being happy because of it. If children are not allowed to make their own choices within the structure set by the parent, how will they learn to make good choices as adults? This is the kind of guidance children need. They don't need the isolation of time-out—it teaches nothing.

Time-out is not the answer to the complexity of human interaction. Raising good kids requires talking to them, explaining the world to them, and setting appropriate limits on their choices. Then they can learn to monitor themselves both now and later in life. Good parenting also involves being aware of the emotional and physical needs (HALTSS) of the child and responding to them in a timely, appropriate manner. Using these tools, parents can banish both the tantrum and the time-out—at the same time!

Chapter 4

Never Remove Toys/Playthings or Important Devices from Your Child

It is important to recognize that taking away a child's toy, iPhone, or any cherished item as punishment for behavior a parent disapproves of reflects a low level of parenting skill. There is simply nothing beneficial about it. Most of us grew up experiencing this kind of discipline. Our toys or beloved possessions were taken away for behavioral infractions. And did any of us like it? Of course not.

The negative fallout of removing prized objects is often resentment and anger directed at the parent. Whatever the child did to prompt the removal of the item fades into the background, and in its place arises low self-esteem and emotional resentment.

It's easy—and tempting—to take things away from a child. For example, a young child might cry because her doll's dress is torn, and the quick reaction might be, *"Stop that crying or I'll take your dolly away."* Or, *"Stop crying or I'll give you something to really cry about."* Even, *"What's wrong with you?"* These are especially tempting responses when a parent is tired or stressed and simply doesn't want to hear crying. But this easy way out leads to one of two outcomes: either the crying intensifies, or the child learns to suppress their feelings in order to get the toy back. The message becomes: *Stop feeling, and you may have your toy returned.* This is a dangerous lesson. Teaching a child not to feel is a profound mistake that results from uninformed or reactive parenting.

So, who pays the price for the parent's inability to handle the child's emotions? The child does. The parent may achieve their short-term goal—getting the child to stop crying about the torn dress—but at the cost of emotional suppression. The removal of the toy becomes a material threat, nothing more and nothing less. It does not help the child learn how to solve emotional problems when they are faced with one.

Let's walk through the example again. The young child is crying because the doll's dress got caught on something and tore. This reaction is normal. If we tear our shirt or dress, we're not happy either. We may not cry, but we certainly feel disappointment or frustration.

Ideally, the parent should empathize with the child's feelings:

"I'm so sorry your doll's dress got torn. Maybe we can find another dress, and I can sew or pin the torn one. I'm sure you're sad this happened. Maybe you're even mad. It's okay to feel that way. It's okay to cry. Let's see what we can do to make it better."

Admittedly, this approach takes more time and involves actual communication. It requires patience, empathy, and attention and problem solving. Sometimes a parent may not be in a position to offer that level of involvement because it is impractical. A shortened, empathetic approach such as *"I can't fix this now, but I promise I will later"* is also acceptable. But often, parents are in a position to respond thoughtfully—and when they are, the best possible outcome is to do so.

Today, many children have personal cell phones, iPads, or computers. These devices serve as primary means of communication with peers, especially when children are home alone after school—a common scenario in households where both parents work. These devices not only offer emotional connection but also physical safety, such as the ability to call 911 in an emergency. They can act as an emotional safety net.

It is critical and of utmost importance that we avoid removing these devices as a form of punishment for behavior we find unacceptable. Taking away a cell phone can create fear and isolation in a child who depends on it to stay connected with friends or family. For some, particularly "only" children or those in strained home environments, losing access to their phone may feel worse than physical punishment. It can induce desperation and/or depression in the child. Parents who remove such devices do not fully understand the emotional consequences of their actions or they wouldn't do it.

Most of us were not raised with the kind of parenting I am advocating. As a result, many people instinctively dismiss this approach as indulgent or foolish—because they never received it themselves. There is a natural tendency to minimize or mock the care we didn't get. Admitting we lacked emotional nurturing is painful, so we deflect that discomfort with sarcasm or judgment and shun the ideas to suppress the feelings as they arise. We often want to defend the parent for their destructive parenting, as this helps avoid painful feelings, such as hurt, anger or sadness.

Growing up as one of eight children, I can tell you there was little room for emotional responsiveness or communication around feelings. We coped, but it wasn't helpful, and it made things harder. I recall long car rides where we would irritate each other, and my father would yell, *"I'll pull over and slap the pair of you if you don't stop fighting!"* We were hot, hungry, cramped and uncomfortable (eight kids in the back of a station wagon including the dog) and the threat was either more delay or less time at the beach. In effect, the punishment was the removal of something desirable—time at the beach.

Empathy would have helped. A statement like, *"I know it's hot, and it's a long drive. Let's talk about what you're excited to do when we get to the beach,"* would have gone a long way. I long for a time when that could have happened—but frankly, it never would have. My father received little good parenting himself, and subsequently, was ill-equipped to effectively raise eight children.

I believe good people want to learn how to better respond to their children. Transforming moments of strife into opportunities for connection can profoundly affect a child's future. Learning how to manage emotions and solve problems forms the basis of a successful emotional life.

Good parenting requires self-awareness and knowing how to make good decisions for our children. We can only make wise decisions when we are in tune with our own emotions—when we can tell whether we're feeling anger, suppressing it, projecting it, or turning it inward into depression. The ability to understand and manage emotions starts in childhood. If we don't teach our children how to deal with feelings, we risk setting them up for a life of emotional dysfunction. Parenting behaviors like spanking, yelling and removing cell phones never teach the lessons of emotional awareness that people need to learn to be happy and successful.

Removing toys or cherished belongings in response to undesirable behavior disrupts this emotional development. It teaches nothing constructive. Instead, it lowers self-esteem, creates anger, and disrupts the parental bond. Children learn that they must –without questioning–do what the parent wants, not what they want. This diminishes authenticity and creates a dysfunctional level of codependency. This is the definition of conditional love. The child absorbs the belief: *I am only lovable when I deny myself and please others, in this case, the parents.*

This mindset is not only damaging in childhood—it's a major contributor to the failure of adult relationships particularly marriage. It is a disturbing fact that two people can get along fairly well until they are married. That's when the trouble begins as it is like a switch is flipped that brings up all the unconscious pain of each partner. The family "starts all over again" and we are met with the difficulties of codependency and fear of abandonment.

Though codependency is often more visible in dysfunctional marriages, it starts in childhood. When a parent withdraws love or access to valued items in response to noncompliance, the child learns that love is contingent. The adult who grows from that child often believes their self-worth depends on constant sacrifice for others.

Children act out. They get bad grades. They're mean to their siblings. But punishing them by removing emotionally significant belongings or for that matter any belongings, damages the parent–child relationship instead of strengthening it. And, even worse, the child learns nothing about how to correct acting out, bad grades or anger at their siblings.

Children see everything. When adults behave irresponsibly, they usually keep their phones, cars, and comforts. Children notice this hypocrisy.

What all people—regardless of age—want is understanding through communication and problem-solving. Teach your children these skills while you still have the chance. The lessons will stay with them for life.

Punishment through the removal of desired objects teaches nothing positive. Worse, it can cause deep emotional harm.

Chapter 5

Never Ground Your Child or Make Your Child Miss Important Events

Grounding is a common parenting tool used mainly for preteens and teenagers. It is, of course, ineffective. Somehow, parents believe that keeping a child at home for perceived "bad behavior" will change their behavior. They assume the child will remember not to repeat the infraction because of the "suffering" caused by staying home for two weeks. In reality, the teen is more likely plotting ways to avoid future punishment while quietly harboring resentment, sadness, and anger. Remorse is unlikely—but a drop in self-esteem is almost certain.

My piano teacher explained to me that in high school, he began to get poor grades. When his report card came in, his parents grounded him for six weeks. During those six weeks, he explained that he did not do a single piece of school work. Deep resentment had set in. A second report card arrived at home with even worse grades, and he was grounded again for a further six weeks. It was at this time he began his journey into drug use and depression. Was the grounding effective? No. Did it create apathy and resentment? Yes. Would it not have been better to talk to the teenager than ground him? Of course. In this scenario, the relationship between drug use and the emotional pain caused by being excessively punished by grounding and the following isolation and lost connection with his peers is clear. Often, the connection is not so easy to see. But I assure you, it is there.

A teenager's behavior can have life-threatening consequences, making it all the more important to maintain a strong emotional bond with them. That bond enables you to help them recognize and navigate the dangers they face. Most films portray teens as sullen, angry, and uncooperative. This depiction is often accurate, especially in the context of divorce. What those films don't show is how the teenager became that way. A teen doesn't act angry and withdrawn simply because they are a teenager. That behavior is often learned—shaped by ineffective parenting during earlier years.

Developmental psychologist Erik Erikson developed a theory called the **Psychosocial Stages of Development**. He believed that personality develops in a sequence of stages, based on what is known as the **epigenetic principle**, which suggests that growth occurs in a predetermined order, influenced by one's environment and community.

The fifth psychosocial stage—**identity vs. role confusion**—takes place during adolescence (ages 12–18). During this period, teens work to establish a sense of personal identity that will guide them for the rest of their lives. Teens need to develop a sense of self. Success in forming this identity leads to the ability to remain true to oneself. Failure may result in a fragile sense of self and role confusion.

When parents encourage personal exploration, teens are more likely to develop a strong sense of identity and internal control. But if parents are authoritarian or excessively controlling, they hinder the adolescent's ability to navigate this critical stage. A teenager cannot resolve the developmental challenge of identity versus role confusion under such restrictive parenting.

According to Erikson, teens primarily develop a sense of identity through **social interaction with their peers**. That's why, as a parent, you may suddenly find you're no longer the center of your child's universe. This shift is developmentally appropriate. It is the work of the teen to develop a strong ego identity. They must discover their own beliefs, values, and ideals. They cannot simply mirror their parents' identities—they need to forge their own.

This developmental phase is often the most challenging for parents, particularly those who have relied on an authoritarian style in the first eleven years of the child's life. In such homes, the child has had their values assigned rather than explored. When adolescence arrives, the natural drive to become one's true self emerges, often appearing as rebellion. It may seem as though your child no longer loves or respects you—but that is not the case. Adolescents who do not go through this process of self-definition are at risk of future instability and dissatisfaction.

Teens look to their peers to help define themselves. They compare and evaluate: *Do I want to be as money-driven as my friend Johnny? Do I want to marry and have five kids? Do I want to be a doctor like my sibling?* Those who skip this process may become aimless and difficult to motivate. A teen cannot become their parent. They must become themselves.

Some parents believe only they know the "right" path for their teen. This belief obstructs the teen's self-exploration and often leads to conflict.

In the film *The Hill*, based on a true story, Dennis Quaid plays Pastor James Hill, the father of future baseball player

Rickey Hill. Rickey, despite facing physical challenges, exhibits extraordinary talent and passion for baseball. However, his father insists that his destiny is to become a preacher. This conflict drives the film's narrative. Ultimately, Rickey's determination prevails—but not before his father's rigid belief system harms both Rickey and the rest of the family, who watch him be demeaned and denied the opportunity to pursue his dream. Pastor Hill thought he knew who Rickey was and what his future should be. He was wrong. And he had no right to assume that he knew what the right life path for Rickey was going to be.

During this stage of development, teens make mistakes. Let's consider some scenarios. If a ten-year-old doesn't make her bed and loses cell phone privileges until she complies, that's one level of a parenting challenge. With teens, the stakes rise dramatically. Suppose your teenager takes the family car, drives under the influence, and stays out past curfew. Now what?

Do we revoke driving privileges? That seems logical. Do we ground them? That might seem appropriate. Do we yell, cry, and claim they're turning our hair gray? Lecture them about the dangers of drunk driving? Shame them by calling them irresponsible? Label them as stupid or selfish?

None of the above is necessary—or effective.

Start by welcoming your teen home and expressing your relief that they are safe. Let them sleep. The next morning, initiate a calm conversation. Ask them to describe what happened and why. This is a moment for compassion, understanding and accountability. Ask how they feel about what they did. Are they afraid? Are they sad? What do they think the repercussions of this behavior could have been?

Did their actions affect others emotionally? Were friends involved in encouraging this behavior?

No shaming, lecturing, or no litanies of things done wrong and no grounding your teen. Avoid punishment rooted in fear or anger, like revoking future prom privileges. These reactions serve the parent's emotional needs—not the child's development.

By **not** relying on punitive techniques, the parent remains emotionally present and available to the child in a difficult situation. This is not to say the behavior is condoned. Parents can also express how they felt: *"I was scared to death you were in a terrible car crash."* Clearly, teens need protection and guidance. That's the job. One can employ solutions that effect change without damaging the parent–child bond.

When I was sixteen years old, I backed our family station wagon into a palm tree at 3:00 a.m. I had been drinking. When I arrived home, I went into my parents' bedroom and told them what had happened. I left the part out about the drinking. The impact of backing into the tree was so intense that it ruined the frame underneath the car, and my father had to sell the vehicle. My parents never asked me any questions or punished me. Knowing that I had created a problem which included financial hardship was enough pain for me and, of course, I never forgot it. I didn't need punishment to know I had made a grave mistake. I was not grounded. I didn't miss the junior prom. The natural consequences were deeply instructive. Although my parents' silence wasn't ideal (a discussion would have been much better), the experience taught me everything I needed to know.

Chapter 6

Never Make Your Child Do Chores Play Is Their Work

Doing chores as a child is generally unpleasant. Children often don't understand why chores need to be done—let alone why they must be the ones to do them.

I must admit I was one of those children. As one of eight siblings—fourth from the eldest—I can attest that there were massive amounts of chores to be done. The truth is, the work was endless. My overworked mother, without any hired help, did most of it. Occasionally, her mother would come stay with us for months at a time. She'd drink black coffee and eat dry toast for breakfast, then spend the day mopping, cleaning, and doing whatever else needed doing. Her visits were a respite for both my mother and me. During those times, I believe we were exempt from dishes and other chores. I liked that.

When I spoke at my mother's funeral, I spoke about being unhappy and somewhat resentful when my mother would request my help. That day, I asked for her forgiveness. Only as an adult could I understand how much she needed help and that the lack of outside help, though needed, was not provided.

She often asked me to hang the laundry in the yard, bring it in once dry, and then fold it. She also wanted me to iron. All eight children wore white shirts and uniforms to school, and those shirts had to be ironed. I did that ironing. Eventually, my mother offered to pay me twenty-five cents for every two shirts I pressed, and that made the task more bearable. I could look forward to spending the money on Saturday at the local soda fountain. It was a big raise, considering my regular allowance was fifty cents a week.

Later, when I was in college, a sorority sister asked me to iron her clothes because she didn't know how. I was stunned. She explained that she had grown up with a full-time housekeeper who did all the family's chores. This was completely foreign to me.

So why do I tell this story?

I believe the notion that children need chores to become functional adults is overstated and misguided. My mother likely believed it was my duty as one of the four daughters to do housework. I don't recall my four brothers participating in those tasks. My mother genuinely needed help, and, being controlled by my father, I believe she was afraid to ask for outside assistance. After all, she was the homemaker, and he worked. This traditional arrangement was hard on all of us. And although I felt sad for my mother's position as homemaker and caregiver for eight children without adequate help, that arrangement was extremely hard on me.

Parents often fear that if they don't assign chores, their children will become spoiled, entitled, or lazy, lacking a solid work ethic. I beg to differ.

Research consistently shows that the work of childhood is play. Play is essential for cognitive, social, emotional, and physical development. Through play, children learn to solve problems, express creativity, and build skills such as cooperation and negotiation. A 2018 report by the American Academy of Pediatrics emphasized that play fosters executive function, planning, self-regulation, and resilience—describing it as a child's "job" in developing foundational abilities.

A small child must engage in play, both alone and with others, to grow into a fully functioning adult. Play is intrinsically motivated, joyful, and free from external pressures. This is the environment we want for our children—one that promotes happiness, autonomy, discovery, and achievement. Building a sandcastle in a sandbox or on a beach is both a creative and satisfying accomplishment. Learning through play is the foundation of childhood.

Soon enough, your children enter school, which becomes their next "job." Success in school is often driven by the expectations of parents and teachers. If a parent believes in their child's ability to succeed, that belief is one of the strongest predictors of achievement. Doing well in school offers its own rewards. But to succeed academically, children also need a stable home. A household filled with fear, conflict, or tension significantly hinders learning.

Because I strongly believed chores were not essential to child development, I never required my son to do them. Although he and I both agree this was a wonderful arrangement, once married his wife did not think so. Despite having some household help, he now shares domestic responsibilities with her as part of a happy, cooperative marriage. It wasn't like he couldn't learn it as an adult. And he did.

Many parents assume that if they don't make their children do chores, the children will grow up inept or selfish. But my son is now an attorney, working long hours in pursuit of his goals. Did he need to do chores to get there? Apparently not. Did he need to do chores as a child to learn how to contribute to household duties as a spouse? Again, no.

In fact, I believe a strong work ethic can be nurtured by *not* forcing children to do chores. Freedom from these burdens allows for unstructured development and preserves a child's sense of autonomy. When children are not coerced, they are more likely to choose work freely later in life.

So how many chores should a child do? My answer is simple: **Let them play**. Encourage unstructured and structured play. And when necessary tasks arise, offer payment as they get older. Payment for older children allows for autonomy and an opportunity to learn about the meaning and managing of money.

Chapter 7

Never Call Your Child Names

One of the easiest things NOT to do as a parent is to call your child names.

Labeling a child in any way can have lifelong and deeply negative implications. If a child hears that they are lazy or unmotivated, that belief can take root and shape the course of their entire life—unless it is addressed and dismantled later through therapy or other effective means.

I recall attending a party at a neighbor's house. The father, his daughter, and I were talking about college and other matters. At one point, the father turned to me and said, in front of his daughter, "She was never really smart enough to get into a good college, so she made do with where she was ultimately accepted." I watched the daughter's face fall, and yet she said nothing in her defense. This sad moment is a perfect example of how a parent can destroy a child's sense of self with an offhand comment. This daughter, now an adult, had likely internalized her father's belief long ago and appeared to accept it as truth.

Although this was a somewhat indirect form of name-calling, it was name-calling all the same. He was essentially labeling her "not smart enough" or "dumb."

Parents often say things they believe to be "truths" or that certain things need to be said in order to set appropriate expectations. When I was in high school, my father told me I could be a nurse, a teacher, or a secretary. "There are only three choices," he said. "Pick one." I wanted to major in music, but that wasn't allowed. It took me years to realize that I had the intelligence and ambition to pursue anything I wanted. Still, the nagging belief that I wasn't smart enough for a career in law, medicine, or business plagued me for most of my life.

The power of a parent's words cannot be overstated. They are enduring and, if negative, profoundly destructive. Looking back, I now view my father's words as misogynistic. At the time, however, he thought he was doing me a favor by outlining what he believed were my "realistic" options or his "truths" about the world. What I actually heard was: *You're just a stupid girl, and this is all that's available to you.* The most heartbreaking part is that I believed him. It took a great deal of work to free myself from that belief.

As Richard Bach wrote, "Argue for your limitations, and they are yours."

There are countless ways parents can label their children, unintentionally planting seeds of self-doubt that last a lifetime:

"You're not very athletic. You're shy. You're a bully. You act like a victim. You don't make friends easily. You're not good at math. You can't spell. You're not artistic like your sister. You have no musical talent. You're lazy, stupid, dumb, mixed up, silly, not serious enough, a troublemaker. You have poor penmanship, poor writing skills, and you're just not good enough."

These statements are often said without a second thought, yet their impact can be profound. It is imperative that parents understand how deeply harmful these labels can be.

All such labels, whether said in jest or in anger, share a common message: *You're not good enough.* And if a child believes they aren't good enough for their own parents, how can they possibly feel worthy in the eyes of others—future friends, coworkers, or even a spouse?

Shaming is often used in a misguided attempt to change a child's behavior. But shame doesn't foster growth; it undermines **self-esteem, motivation, and success**.

Many of these parental put-downs stem from a fear that the child will become too arrogant, too proud, or too full of themselves. In my family, we were taught that having a "big head" was a cardinal sin. It meant you thought you were more than you really were. Instead, we were expected to remain humble—more accurately, ashamed—and to remember that we were sinners from birth. The idea that we had inherent value was never part of the message. We knew we had faults, but we had no idea what it meant to be "good enough," because that standard was never defined—only implied.

Clinical psychologist and educator Haim Ginott wisely said, "Even in fun, labeling can be disabling. Labels often put children in a box they feel they can't get out of. Labels are like price tags—they stick, and they're hard to remove. To reduce a complex, growing human being to "you're stupid" is to trap them in a mental prison with no clear exit."

Ginott advises parents and teachers to address **what a child does**, not **who the child is**. This preserves self-esteem and encourages growth. A parent might say, "I see your toys are still on the floor," rather than, "You're always so messy." A teacher might say, "I see you're having trouble sitting still," instead of, "You're always so disruptive."

I've observed that many people have difficulty praising others—especially their children. This often stems from the fact that they never received unconditional love themselves. For example, an angry parent might have said, "If you don't do your homework, you'll never amount to anything." Hearing "you'll never amount to anything" can echo inside a child's mind for a lifetime.

Our inner child—the subconscious mind—doesn't disappear with age. It continues to long for love and praise. If that inner child is still hurting, it may be incredibly difficult for a parent to praise others, including their own children. The inner child feels deprived and empty—and that emptiness makes it painful to recognize or express admiration for someone else.

Even when a parent consciously recognizes a child's good behavior or talents, the **inner child** may refuse to cooperate. The praise simply won't come. It's too painful. It feels unfair. It feels impossible.

This is why we must recognize that **knowing** what to do as a parent—praise instead of criticize—may not be enough. We also have to **heal ourselves**.

Yes, parenting strategies and skill-building matter. If they didn't, I wouldn't be writing this book. Serious child abuse and poor parenting still persist in our society— sometimes not because people don't know better, but because they haven't healed their own emotional wounds.

The single greatest gift we can give our children is a healed, emotionally secure version of ourselves.

In addition to learning effective parenting techniques, we must also do the inner work that allows us to pass on not only knowledge but **emotional wholeness**. That's the foundation our children need to grow, thrive, and become the best versions of themselves. (See Chapter 20.)

Chapter 8

Never Say Anything Negative of Any Kind About Your Child

It is important to always remember the power a parent holds to either help a child build high self-esteem or, conversely, to diminish or debilitate it. Offhanded remarks can have long-lasting consequences. For example, if your child is having difficulty with a task, and you say in front of other siblings, "Oh, it always takes you longer to finish things," or "You sure are slow with your homework," those comments—though seemingly minor—are unnecessary and harmful. When heard often enough, they embed themselves in the subconscious. The child may come to believe they are simply "slow"—that this is an unchangeable flaw because the parent said so.

When you place a limitation on your child, that belief can spill into other areas of their life. What starts as a comment about homework may later manifest as insecurity at work or in relationships. The child doesn't just believe they are slow at schoolwork—they believe they are slow, period.

It is especially tempting to speak about a child's shortcomings when they are very young, under the mistaken belief that they are not yet capable of understanding. For example, you might be chatting with friends at the park while your toddler has trouble engaging with other children. You might say, "Well, Johnny has always been shy and is afraid of other kids." If your child is within earshot, they've heard you. And if they hear that kind of comment enough, it becomes a belief they internalize: *I am shy. I am afraid. I am different. I am less than.*

And once you begin speaking negatively about your child in early childhood, you're more likely to continue doing it as they grow. That's why our awareness of the things we say about our children—especially in front of them—must be at the highest level. Offhanded or, worse, intentional negative comments have no place in healthy parenting.

This rule applies throughout the entire span of your relationship with your child—from birth into adulthood. Even young adults can be hurt by well-intentioned but shaming remarks from a parent.

In Chapter 7, I referenced a father who, while speaking with me in the presence of his adult daughter, said she was "never smart enough" to get into a good college and had to settle for wherever she was accepted. Though not directly calling her names, his words were effectively saying she was "not smart enough" or "too dumb to excel." Even if the father had a story he wanted to share, discussing this in front of his daughter was poor parenting. (See Chapter 9.)

Even if it were true that his daughter lacked the academic profile for an Ivy League school, was it necessary to say it out loud—especially in her presence? Is it ever necessary to focus on the negative when talking about your children? No. I was shocked by his statement. It was clear she was hurt, and yet the father showed no awareness of the emotional impact. But lack of awareness is not an excuse. As parents, it is our responsibility to be conscious of how our words affect our children—at every age.

I remember my father once saying, in front of my brother, that he was bad at math. My brother didn't even flinch. He had heard it so many times it had become a fixed belief. I believed it too—about him and about myself, though I don't recall hearing it directed at me. Still, I carried the belief for years until I disproved it by studying diligently for the GRE and scoring high on the math section. I *could* do math. I had just never believed it.

In my father's case, he excelled at math, and I suspect he didn't want his children to surpass him. In fact, this attitude seemed to apply across the board. Though never stated outright, it felt like it was forbidden to outshine our father.

There are many unconscious forces that influence our parenting. We may not even be aware of them. If you had asked my father whether he wanted all eight of his children to succeed, he would have said yes without hesitation. But his unconscious need to be better than us often undercut that stated desire.

It's possible some of us have done a version of this to our own children.

This is why the rule against negative comments is so critical. Saying hurtful things about our children is a parenting error that can be corrected with relatively little effort. You don't need years of therapy to stop making critical or hurtful remarks. Amazingly, you can simply stop. We all can have full control over this behavior.

What helps us make this change is understanding the lasting damage that negative comments can cause. They lower a child's self-esteem. They create resentment, anger, sadness, and alienation. The best way to grasp their impact is to recall any negative comments your own parents made about you. If you can remember them, it's likely because they hurt. Being called "stupid," "lazy," "unmotivated," or "not good enough" can shape a person's sense of self for a lifetime.

This is a rule without exception: **Expressing negative beliefs about your children in their presence is unjustifiable and unnecessary.**

Stopping this behavior—entirely—will strengthen and protect your relationship with your child.

Chapter 9

Never Publicly Shame Your Child

Public shaming is a dreadful experience for any child. Children, above all, seek the love and approval of their parents. This approval is not merely emotional—it is essential for their survival.

Children must form strong attachments to their parents or caregivers, or they cannot thrive. Attachment and authenticity are two of the most vital components of childhood development. All children begin life as authentic human beings, crying when necessary to get their needs met. This is their survival mechanism, and, without interference, they use it effectively. A child will scream and cry until they get the attention of their parents. While parents may find this behavior frustrating, it is actually a blessing—not a curse. Without it, how would they know when to feed the baby, change the baby's diaper, or tend to pain or distress?

As children grow and become more self-sufficient, their attachment needs evolve to include approval and recognition. Children want to feel that they are the center of their parents' emotional universe—and they need to be. Good parenting means holding your children at the heart of your emotional life.

Reality dictates that we must work and provide for our families, and this requires time and energy. But even working parents can build strong emotional relationships with their children through praise, communication, and teaching. These expressions of love and connection must be age appropriate and delivered in a positive manner. In doing so, children develop a positive sense of self—one that supports a fulfilling and emotionally stable life.

Unfortunately, many parents mistakenly believe that criticizing their children in front of others is an effective disciplinary tool. They may assume that offering critical remarks in front of a sibling or peer will increase the impact and encourage the child to change.

Nothing could be further from the truth.

The only result of public criticism is internalized shame and growing resentment toward the parent. When I was a senior in high school, my father would often make comments at the dinner table about how I was not living up to the standards set by my two older sisters. The fact that I can remember these incidents so clearly more than fifty years later reveals just how deep the wounds of public shaming can go. I have never forgotten those remarks. My mother said nothing. She did not defend me. This silence was part of our family dynamic—and one that affected each of my siblings at one point or another.

Acquiescence in the shaming is as harmful as the original remark. In fact, when a parent allows such harm to continue unchallenged, they are just as responsible as the one delivering the abuse. This may be difficult to accept, but it is a truth worth understanding. A parent who fails to protect a child from verbal, physical or emotional harm— especially when they have the power to intervene—is complicit in that harm.

Typically, children direct their resentment toward the parent who actively abuses them, while excusing the silent parent. Sometimes, children even view the silent parent as a fellow victim. And, to be fair, the silent parent may be operating from a place of fear. But fear is not an excuse when the well-being of a child is at stake. It is always a parent's job to protect their child. Yes, it is a high demand to place on a mother who is herself being abused. But she must find help. She must find a way.

As with corporal punishment, I believe that shaming and criticism are tools used by parents to exert domination and control. When a child's self-esteem is compromised, the child often becomes more malleable—more likely to obey, more likely to suppress. But the long-term consequences can be devastating. Rage and emotional abuse may later erupt in adult relationships, whether in marriage, friendship, or the workplace. An excessively controlling boss, for instance, may be acting out the fallout of childhood shame and domination.

The unchecked power of an emotionally unaware parent is dangerous. A parent may project their own shame, anger, or unresolved trauma onto a child as a way to rid themselves of those painful emotions. Becoming conscious of your own inner world as a parent—your feelings, your motives, your pain—is your responsibility. Children are defenseless against projections of this kind. They do not deserve to carry the emotional burden of their parent's wounds. They are innocent. When this kind of projection occurs, children can become the unwitting carrier of pain that is not even their own.

It is possible to change the world—one child at a time—by unconditionally loving and protecting our children. We do this by rejecting shame, embracing awareness, and by following these twenty rules.

Chapter 10

Never Make Your Child Share His or Her Toys

When my son—now thirty-three years old—was about four, I attended a lecture at his elementary school. The guest speaker was Educator Bev Bos.

I recall her saying many insightful things that day about child-rearing, but the one that struck me most profoundly was her assertion that parents should **not** force their children to share their toys with siblings or others.

At the time, this sounded like self-serving heresy. It seemed that all parents of young children were obsessed with getting them to share. In fact, parents I knew were so obsessed that if their children did not share, it was practically the mark of the devil. Sharing was viewed as a moral benchmark—a measure of whether their child was "good" or "bad"—and certainly as a predictor of future success in both personal and professional relationships.

In fact, just the other day I was watching the news when one of the anchors began speaking about his own children. He mentioned that his young daughter refused to share her toys, and this deeply upset him. He felt something must be wrong with her—some inherent character flaw—and he even planned to bring the issue up with her pediatrician.

Watching him express such concern over what is developmentally normal prompted me to return to this book, which I had set aside some time ago. I couldn't help but question how a highly educated, worldly young man could be so far from the truth about parenting. I was alarmed and began to realize that, fundamentally, many parents have little idea how to raise a happy, healthy child. Too often, their only tools are punishments—harsh, alienating measures inflicted on children who are desperate for love, attention, and approval.

In defense of these parents, psychologically sound and accessible parenting knowledge is surprisingly hard to come by. Most have never been taught a better way.

Suffice it to say, if your child does not want to share their toys with others, this is not the mark of the devil. They are simply like all young children: naturally and appropriately egocentric. This self-centeredness is not a flaw—it is a normal survival mechanism.

I'm not sure where the idea of forced sharing originated. Perhaps in earlier times, when toys or belongings were scarce, it seemed necessary. But that is no longer the case for most American families. A parent today can visit a thrift store or library and easily find toys and books for their children to enjoy.

When someone asks me, "But why shouldn't my child share their toys or books?" I respond with a question of my own: "Would you loan your brand-new Ferrari to the teenager next door?" Most people laugh and admit they wouldn't dream of letting a teenager speed down their street in their new car.

"Well," I say, "it's no different for a two-year-old with a new dolly or toy train." That item is theirs. They own it.

And they are free to choose whether or not to share it. No obligation. No coercion.

So, what should a parent do about the sibling who wants to play with that particular toy?

Bev Bos suggested that while the child is playing with their toy, the parent can read a book or engage in another activity with the child who wants the coveted toy. She also suggested comforting the child who doesn't have the toy. "I am so sorry you can't play with that other child's toy right now because it is theirs. Let's find another toy for you to enjoy.

Often—but not always—the child who was reluctant to share will eventually bring their toy over to join in the fun.

I'm fairly certain this misguided idea of forced sharing remains widespread in preschools and early childhood development centers. I hope we can collectively begin to understand that pressuring children to share is as inappropriate—and ultimately harmful—as yelling or grounding.

Both practices ignore what children actually need: respect, empathy, autonomy, and the opportunity to develop at their own pace.

Chapter 11

Never Punish Your Child or Make Him or Her say "Sorry"

It is important to understand that Skinnerian principles of behavior dictate that punishment only suppresses the unwanted behavior in the presence of the punisher. Because of this fundamental law of human behavior, once the punisher is absent, the behavior is likely to resume. Naturally, this is not the goal of most parents when they punish their child. They mistakenly believe that punishment leads to lasting behavioral change. This belief is incorrect and has been disproven repeatedly in psychological studies.

In the psychological literature, punishment is categorized as either **positive** (adding an undesirable stimulus) or **negative** (removing a desirable stimulus). An example of positive punishment would be assigning extra chores or scolding a child. In essence, something is being added. Negative punishment might involve taking away a toy or a desired activity due to perceived misbehavior—removing something of value.

This system is ineffective in creating long-term behavioral change. A child may comply in the presence of the punishing parent but is likely to act out independently when that parent is absent. If you want to raise an honest, emotionally healthy adult, punishment is not the answer.

Punishment can engender resentment and aggression toward the parents, and often later, rebellion. In earlier decades, many American teenagers left home at sixteen or seventeen, frequently to escape harsh and sometimes physically abusive parents. Usually, these parents also grew up under an abusive, tyrannical system that was believed to be "good and effective" parenting. Punishment does not support strong or loving parent–child relationships.

One of Walt Disney's biographers describes Disney's father, Elias, as a physical abuser whose frequent use of corporal punishment severely damaged Walt's relationship with him. Walt reportedly wondered how such a "cruel old man" could be his father and questioned why his mother never intervened. Elias valued hard manual labor over play and dismissed Walt's interests in drawing and animals as frivolous. His punishments were said to be severe, even by the standards of the era where striking your child was the norm. He would use a switch on all four of his sons for the smallest infractions. Walt's older brothers, Herbert and Raymond, left home as soon as possible, leaving Walt and Roy to endure the brunt of their father's brutality. As an adult, Walt reportedly created Disneyland's Main Street to give children a place where they could feel happy, safe, and secure—if only for a moment. He called it "the happiest place on Earth." Sadly, that was not the kind of home Walt and Roy experienced.

Punishment also instills anxiety and fear of the punisher rather than discouraging the unwanted behavior itself. Frequent or harsh punishment damages the parent–child bond and may impair the child's ability to form healthy relationships later in life.

Parents often ask, "If I can't punish my child, what am I supposed to do? I thought discipline was essential in raising responsible members of society and in helping children learn right from wrong."

Children of all ages will be punished by the natural consequences of life and do not need "extra punishment" for them to learn. If a child chooses not to study for a spelling test, they will likely receive a poor grade. If a teenager goes out drinking, the hangover—and potentially the loss of trust or friendships—becomes the natural consequence. These experiences teach valuable lessons without the need for additional punishment. Children do not need further recrimination from the parents to know that these behaviors are not favorable.

So, what *do* children need? They need communication and understanding when their behavior is unacceptable to the parent. For example, a sibling may hit the other sibling because of some disagreement between them. The sibling who hit the other needs communication from the parent. This communication can be simply:

"In this family, we use our words to say how we feel. We do not hit. Hitting is not acceptable in our family. You are part of this family and so you do not hit your sibling."

This is a communication with a set boundary. Communications of this kind must be precise, definitive and clear. In other words, the child may not do this again in this family. It is not punishment—it is communication and a learning opportunity.

Understanding can follow. If the child hit a sibling because their toy was taken, the parent can express empathy:

"I understand you're upset that your sister took your toy. You feel angry and hurt." Children respond well to this kind of emotional validation. In many cases, the sister may then return the toy. If not, she may also need help expressing her feelings. It is possible that the sister won't return the toy because she is feeling resentful or angry about something else. Again, it is the parents place to help the sister express why she doesn't want to return the toy. She can tell her brother what she feels and now you are teaching communication in real time and teaching them how to develop a high level of emotional intelligence, not just enforcing compliance. Remember, punishment does not teach empathy or communication; it teaches resentment.

Emotional intelligence is the ability to manage and understand one's own emotions as well as the emotions of others. Psychologist Daniel Goleman popularized this concept in his 1995 book *Emotional Intelligence: Why It Can Matter More Than IQ*. Emotionally intelligent individuals possess self-awareness, emotional regulation, self-expression, and empathy.

Teaching emotional intelligence often requires active, direct parental involvement. Over time, and through repeated guidance, children learn to communicate effectively on their own.

During these learning moments, it is crucial not to force your child to apologize. While this may sound heretical, insisting on an apology is usually ineffective. Most children are not genuinely sorry when coerced into saying it. Instead, they learn to suppress their true feelings and become less authentic. If a child feels justified in their behavior—say, kicking a friend who they believe wronged them—forcing an apology undermines their sense of emotional integrity. Making your child say they are sorry is insisting that they have feelings that they do not have.

Most children are not sorry in a squabble or fight with another child. There is nothing wrong with that. Teaching a child about their feelings means you are having them talk about being scared, hurt, sad or mad. Children might end up apologizing for something if it's voluntarily, but by no means is it necessary. Forced apologies are inauthentic, create resentment, and damage trust. They may seem to resolve a situation on the surface, but they do not teach accountability or empathy. A child who is made to apologize typically hangs their head and mumbles the words. Why? Because they know they are being forced to lie about their feelings.

This collective cultural expectation—that a child should always say they're sorry—is deeply ingrained, but its purpose is to benefit the adult more than the child. In these cases, the adult doesn't really have to deal with what is really going on between the two children. The adult or parent can just be the judge and jury without all the evidence. They can decide on the guilty party without finding out what really went on. It allows the adult to feel the matter is "settled," even though the child has not learned anything meaningful from the experience.

If punishment were truly effective, recidivism rates among former inmates would be significantly lower. According to a 2018 U.S. Department of Justice study, approximately 68 percent of state prisoners are re-arrested within three years of release—and the rate rises significantly over time. I am not suggesting we eliminate prisons; they are necessary. But we must recognize that trauma, neglect, or untreated mental illness are often what land people there in the first place—and that punishment alone does not create long-term behavioral change.

Today, the sheer number of people living on the streets tells us that our mental health system is in crisis. While temporary financial hardship may account for some homelessness, many unhoused individuals are addicts with untreated mental illness. Though I don't claim to have a comprehensive solution, I do believe that most people in these situations grew up in abusive, violent homes. Their early trauma plays a significant role in their current condition.

Physical punishment, increasingly recognized as a form of violence, consistently predicts negative behavioral outcomes in children. Research shows that it contributes to behavior problems and is not associated with any positive long-lasting results.

Physical punishment as a parenting tool must be eliminated.

THE ALWAYS

PARENTING | THE RULES

*Timeless principles for raising
exceptional children with
unwavering love and guidance*

Parenting: The Rules by Susan M. Thomson, PhD

Chapter 12

Always Praise Your Child

I begin this chapter by stating that praise is a valuable parenting tool—but only when used intentionally and with understanding. It is more complex than simply saying, "Good boy."

In *Punished by Rewards*, author Alfie Kohn argues that praising or rewarding children to elicit specific behaviors can suppress their intrinsic motivation. He contends that children are born with natural curiosity and wonder about the world, and when adults use external rewards to drive behaviors that children would otherwise do willingly, they disrupt this innate process and risk harming the child's development.

Reward-based systems also risk creating what Kohn refers to as "approval attachment"—a form of codependency in which a child becomes reliant on parental praise. If a child is consistently met with "Good boy!" after completing tasks, they may begin to pursue only those actions that earn approval, growing fearful when the praise is withheld. Over time, their self-worth becomes contingent on external validation and the child's life begins to revolve around getting praise or approval from the parent. This dynamic can result in an adult with low self-esteem, poor boundaries, and people-pleasing tendencies.

Ironically, a child whose behavior is tightly controlled through praise may grow up to be controlling themselves.

Approval attachment can also be created through rigid limit-setting, such as: "You may never drink, smoke, or have sex until you are twenty-one." The problem arises when a child or adolescent breaks one of these rules and the parent responds by withdrawing love, affection, or emotional support. This form of emotional abandonment is profoundly damaging to the child's psychological well-being. It teaches the child that love is conditional and only available when they comply with expectations.

Any kind of abandonment, especially the withdrawal of love, is feared by the child and harms the parent–child relationship. The child may grow into an adult who struggles in intimate relationships—particularly in marriage, where fear of abandonment is often a key barrier to honest communication. Such adults may suppress their needs or feelings to avoid the perceived threat of being left.

Thus, both praise and limit-setting are far more nuanced than they appear. These tools are often misused when employed to control behavior rather than to foster connection, growth, and self-awareness.

All children crave the admiration, support, and unconditional love of their parents. They need to feel that they are the most important part of their parents' emotional world—and they should be. Some might consider this an unrealistic demand. But ask yourself: Would you have liked your parents to have valued you fully and expressed how important and loved you were? If your answer is no, it's likely you didn't receive this level of affirmation—and that in itself is telling.

The ideal parent offers love without requiring performance. A child should be valued not for achievements but simply for existing.

At a three-day retreat led by John Bradshaw, I witnessed the profound impact of such affirming messages. During one exercise, Bradshaw invited participants to close their eyes and imagine themselves as infants hearing the words: *"Welcome to the world. We are so glad you are here. You are the most important thing in the world to us."* As he repeated these words, I was genuinely surprised as the room filled with many participants sobbing, often loudly. Many of the adults in attendance had never received anything close to this kind of affirmation from their own parents. Sadly, that is more common than not.

While most parents express unconditional love for their infants, this can shift as the child grows, begins to talk, assert independence, and—inevitably—say no. The once-adorable infant becomes a defiant toddler, kicking you in the shin. Ah, this is where the fun begins!

So, what does effective praise actually look like? We certainly don't want to suppress a child's natural drive to learn and explore. In line with Kohn's ideas, praise in educational settings must be used thoughtfully. A teacher, for instance, might recognize a student's achievement and ask, "How do you feel about the work you did?" or "What was it like to get 100 percent on your spelling test?" Instead of saying, "Great job, or good boy" a better approach is to help the child reflect on their own satisfaction with their efforts.

If a student performs poorly, a teacher should avoid public shaming—such as a large red "D" at the top of a paper—and instead speak with the student privately: "How do you feel about this grade? Is there anything I can do to help next time?" This communicates compassion and a willingness to support, rather than judgment.

Most teachers probably do not operate in this way. Still, the goal of education—like parenting—should be to foster resilience and self-worth, not to impose fear and reward compliance. Teachers, like parents, need tools and strategies that promote long-term growth and emotional intelligence. Authoritarianism, punishment for misbehavior, and loud praise for the "good" student is most likely the norm. However, there are better ways to teach children and to essentially be a "third co-parent' in raising happy, fulfilled children,

At home, praise can follow similar principles. Instead of using vague statements like "Good job," parents can become more observant and specific. For example:

"I noticed you made your bed this morning. That must feel good to have it done early—it's a great way to start the day."

In this scenario, you are "catching your child being good." Awareness of the language you are using to praise can make all the difference. It is always a good idea to start your sentences with "I notice that" as you then follow that with describing a behavior rather than labeling a child in a particular way. For example, "I notice that you put your books away" rather than "good boy." In fact, Alfie Kohn says that when he hears someone say "good boy" he wants to reply with "woof."

This type of praise highlights behavior without tying it to personal value. The child understands that the parent approves, but the praise isn't conditional. If the child doesn't make the bed, the best approach may be to ignore it initially. If noncompliance continues, turn it into a joint activity. Make it fun. Add humor. Tasks become more palatable when paired with affection and shared experiences.

Above all, we want to raise children who believe they are worthy not because they obey but because they exist.

When we associate a child's actions with their worth, we risk creating a deeply harmful narrative: *"I am only good when I do what pleases others."* Instead, we must raise children who know: *"I am good because I am."*

A corollary to praise is setting limits. Although this idea has been discussed in other chapters, it bears repeating here. Limit-setting works best when it follows the same model. With praise, we encourage desired behaviors with particular language like "I notice that.". With limits, we do the same—without resorting to punishment or withdrawing love.

A useful phrase to frame family values is: *"In this family..."* For example:

"In this family, we don't hit each other. We use words to express our feelings."

If one child insults another, you might say:

"In this family, we don't call each other names. We talk about how we feel—hurt, angry, sad, or afraid."

Such statements communicate boundaries clearly and without shame.

When my son was in high school, we developed a set of rules that reflected our values and concerns. We told him: "No blackouts, no brownouts, no brothels, and no drunk driving." Not using drugs was already well understood, as he had a near-fatal allergic reaction to codeine as a child. The other rules addressed alcohol and sexual conduct— with a bit of humor. "No brothels" meant no girls in the bed in our home. All his friends also heard this mantra; it was clear and consistent.

By this stage, I no longer needed to preface limits with "In this family." His academic and athletic performance was excellent, so we didn't impose academic-related rules. While not every rule was followed perfectly, we did not respond to rule-breaking with withdrawal of love or affection. We had honest discussions but never equated misbehavior with unworthiness. This distinction is crucial—and transformative.

We must always separate behavior from identity. Your child is not *bad* because they broke a rule. They are still whole, lovable, and deserving of your presence and care.

Alfie Kohn offers several guidelines for more effective praise:

1. **Praise actions, not people.** Don't say, "Good boy." Say, "I liked the way you cleaned up your toys."

2. **Be specific.** Instead of "Great job," say, "I noticed how carefully you painted the picture."

3. **Be sincere.** Avoid praise as manipulation. It must be honest and thoughtful.

4. **Avoid comparisons.** It's preferable not to say, "You did better than the other kids." Instead, ask, "How do you feel about your grade?"

Ultimately, praise and limit-setting are most powerful when used not to control—but to connect. Done well, they help a child build a resilient identity, emotional intelligence, and authentic self-worth.

Chapter 13

Always Expect the Best from Your Child

Many studies have shown that if you expect success from a student or child, you are far more likely to get it. In psychology, this is known as the **Pygmalion effect**—a phenomenon in which higher expectations lead to improved performance. In other words, people tend to live up to—or down to—the expectations set for them. This is especially true for children. Once an expectation is firmly in place, the subconscious begins to align with that expectation.

The term *Pygmalion effect* was coined by psychologists Robert Rosenthal and Lenore Jacobson. In 1968, they conducted a study on the effect of teacher expectations on student performance. Working in an elementary school, they randomly selected students and falsely told their teachers that these students were identified—through a fabricated test—as "academic bloomers."

Due to the teachers' increased expectations, over time, these students showed significant academic improvement. The researchers concluded that the students' higher performance was due to the additional attention, encouragement, and belief they received from their teachers. These findings were published in *Pygmalion in the Classroom*, where Rosenthal and Jacobson demonstrated that belief in potential can shape outcomes—a textbook example of a **self-fulfilling prophecy**.

In this case, better results came directly from higher expectations.

A parent must hold a strong internal belief that their child is capable of success—because when they do, it often becomes true. If a parent fears failure, the child is just as likely to fulfill that expectation.

This message of success is transmitted both consciously and unconsciously. A conscious expression might sound like: *"I believe in you. I know you have what it takes to succeed."* Parents can also offer reassurance by saying, *"If you have any doubts, I'll help you work through them."* This kind of encouragement is generally well received and deeply influential.

Parenting during the so-called dark ages of the 1950s was governed by a set of unspoken rules that were widely accepted across families and communities in the United States. Chief among them was the idea that children should never be allowed to get a "big head" or "big ego." Children were expected to submit to authority so they could grow into obedient, respectable citizens.

Comparisons among siblings were common, and the less capable or lower-performing child often suffered under the weight of these comparisons. Children were expected to "knuckle under" and accept their place in the family hierarchy. Corporal punishment—including spanking and the use of belts—was considered standard practice. Today, we recognize this as physical abuse. Yet the adage *"spare the rod, spoil the child"* was culturally dominant—and still persists in some circles today (see Chapter One).

These false and outdated beliefs turn the parent into a tyrant rather than a cheerleader—when in fact, the child needs someone who stands beside them, always expecting the best.

It's important to note that **unconscious beliefs**—both about ourselves and our children—can be far more powerful than the words we say out loud. If a parent fears that the child may one day surpass them in success, they may, whether intentionally or not, begin to undermine that child's belief in themselves. A parent with low self-esteem may unconsciously pass that insecurity onto their child. If a parent truly believes—however subtly—that their child is inadequate, it may eventually become true.

Children are often defenseless against this kind of psychological influence. They may sense that something is wrong, but lack the awareness or vocabulary to identify it.

Expectations are not limited to academic success. Parents model expectations through their own behavior. A parent who is honest, who doesn't cheat or steal, and who treats others with compassion, teaches a child to do the same. If a parent holds true to their values under pressure, the child learns how to stay honest in difficult situations. If a parent openly discusses their feelings, the child learns that expressing emotions is healthy and acceptable.

In short, we must be the best version of ourselves if we want our children to rise to their full potential.

And we must expect the best from them—no matter what.

Chapter 14

Always Provide Abundantly for Your Child

(Teach Abundance, Not Scarcity)

"L.O.V. E. - Listen. Observe. Validate. Explore."

In *The Ascent of Man*, Jacob Bronowski describes how early humans stood upright in the field to gain a better view of what was coming—either to detect threats or to locate prey. After living on all fours, one of the pivotal advances toward the development of the species *Homo sapiens* was the shift to standing upright, which not only provided safety and food, but also freed the hands to interact with the environment. This interaction between hand and brain was instrumental in shaping who we are today. The opposable thumb enabled early humans to manipulate objects and thus evolve more fully into complex beings.

From this, and multiple studies on enhanced learning experiences for young children, we understand that an enriched environment is crucial for a child's healthy cognitive development. Whether the environment takes the form of toys from Neiman Marcus or the Salvation Army is immaterial. What matters is the **variety and quality of stimulation** available to the child. This includes toys, games, books, art supplies (pens, paper, crayons), music, and opportunities for creative exploration. Outdoor experiences—such as playing in the sandbox, visiting animal parks, or going to museums—also contribute to enriching the child's environment. Even a single trip to Disneyland can create lasting joy and memories and an enriched childhood experience.

Newborns who are left alone in cribs in institutional settings, without meaningful interaction from caregivers, often become cognitively and emotionally impaired—and in extreme cases, may even die. This tragic outcome results from a lack of the stimulation required to develop both the thinking brain and the emotional brain. When critical periods of development are missed in infancy, the effects can be lifelong and largely irreversible.

This institutional example may seem extreme, but it serves to illustrate an important point: sufficient stimulation and learning are essential and fall squarely within the parent's responsibilities. Enriching the home environment in as many ways as possible helps ensure that a child's developmental needs are met.

Reading aloud to your child from the earliest age is one of the most impactful ways to support early learning and language development. Children's television shows may also be enriching, though with one important caveat: the screen must never consistently replace the parent. Watching with your child and discussing what you see can become a shared learning experience.

Withholding toys or activities because you "don't want them to have too many" is, frankly, misguided. There is no such thing as "too many," unless you are using toys as a substitute for your presence. In that case, even one toy may be too many. Otherwise, feel free to indulge. Teach your children a belief in **abundance**, not **scarcity**. Show them that the world will provide—not that they must constantly go without. Withholding positive experiences, affection, or material support sends the wrong message. You can never give too many hugs, too many kisses, or too much love.

When children are given to abundantly, they are more likely to live abundantly.

An **unconscious belief in an abundant universe** can be cultivated in childhood through consistent care and provision. A parent who believes in "not enough"—in scarcity—also transmits that belief, consciously or not. Children absorb this worldview and may carry it into adulthood, where it can quietly sabotage their ability to create success, generate wealth, or live joyfully.

In some cases, religious teachings may complicate this message. For example, Matthew 19:24 contains the metaphor: *"It is easier for a camel to pass through the eye of a needle than for a rich man to enter the kingdom of heaven."* This verse has often been interpreted to mean that wealth and virtue are incompatible. In truth, the message cautions against the **obsessive and sole pursuit of money**, which can obstruct spirituality and moral clarity.

But abundance is a **spiritual concept**, one that includes financial well-being—but is not limited to it. One may inherit wealth but lack fulfillment, meaningful relationships, or inner peace. Abundance, in its truest sense, is the belief—both conscious and unconscious—that the world or universe will provide for you whatever you believe you deserve, across all aspects of life. If your young children grow up in a world where abundance is the norm, they are much more likely to create that for themselves as adults.

The earlier your child learns this, the better. Teach abundance young and help change the children of the world in one generation.

Chapter 15

Always Provide Positive <u>Supervised</u> Social Interactions for Your Child

When my son was four years old, we were living in a two-story home in California, having recently moved from Louisiana. He met a playmate from across the street—let's call him Joey—who was a few years older. We were delighted that there was a child nearby for our son to play with, and the convenience was ideal.

My husband and I had met Joey's parents, who seemed very nice. Being new to the neighborhood, we were eager to build good relationships with those around us. At the time, we were unaware that their son had emotional difficulties, including a diagnosis of ADHD.

One day, we invited Joey over, and he and my son were playing in my son's room. I assumed it was safe to leave them briefly while I took a quick shower—it wasn't their first playdate, and even with only one child, it can be difficult to find time for the things you need to do.

My son's room was upstairs, but generally safe. He was a cautious child who didn't take unnecessary risks. After finishing my shower and getting dressed, I passed by the bedroom and didn't hear any talking or playing. Concerned, I went downstairs to look for them.

What I saw next was alarming.

Outside, Joey was on the second-story balcony, attempting to hoist my son from the ground below. He had tied a rope around my son's waist, and my son was standing on top of our outdoor glass table.

I screamed, "STOP!" Both boys looked at me in surprise. Joey had been working hard to lift my son up to the second floor, and fortunately, he hadn't succeeded. I never determined where they found the rope—likely the garage—but I made sure it was never seen again.

There is often a fine line between being a "helicopter parent" and providing necessary oversight and safety. In this case, I would have done better to lean toward being a helicopter parent.

Afterward, I had an emphatic conversation with both boys about the dangers of what they were doing. After the traumatizing event—at least from my perspective—I sent Joey home.

I share this story because social interaction is essential for children. However, we must be aware of who our children are interacting with and what kind of supervision is appropriate. When I was growing up in a large family of eight children, we had little to no supervision. I once asked my older sister, "How did we survive?" She laughed and said, "I think we just ran wild!" I came through it relatively unscathed, but the world we grew up in at least appeared relatively safe. Today, we live in a different and arguably less safe world.

After that incident, structured play with parental oversight was the only way our son could play with Joey. Everyone understood the new terms. I don't think my son was afraid until he saw the fear in my eyes. He was simply too young to know better, and Joey was too forceful to resist.

I tell this story also to underscore that children can hurt one another when left unsupervised. Social interaction is crucial—but it must be monitored.

Later, we moved to a new house next door, which had a fenced backyard. As a housewarming gift, our realtor who lived behind us asked if I wanted a new kitchen appliance or a gate connecting our backyards, so my son could play with their children. We chose the connecting gate. They had four boys, two were close in age to our son. That gate swung open and closed almost every day, providing him with regular companionship. While the playtimes weren't incident-free, they were largely safe, and supervision was consistent in both homes.

My husband and I made efforts to create an environment that encouraged social interaction and fun. We were fortunate to have the means to provide a trampoline, a makeshift clubhouse, a batting cage, and even a skate ramp—both of which my husband built himself. I'm not sure the neighbors appreciated the aesthetics, but our son's joy and happiness took precedence.

If a location was needed for a school event, we offered our yard. We hosted our son's sixteenth birthday party in our front yard—tent included. We invited parents to assist with supervision and even had a security guard at the gate. Teenagers need just as much, if not more, parental involvement as younger children.

We did all this to enhance our son's opportunities for friendship and enjoyment. My husband and I have always believed in the value of both.

It is the responsibility of parents to provide their children with ample opportunities for fun and friendship. Whether at a public park or a luxury hotel, the setting is less important than the experience itself. Creating shared moments of joy strengthens the bond between parent and child.

Too many parents believe they must "discipline" their children to make them good people. In truth, good people are raised through love, care, time, and attention.

Sports and other extracurricular activities are also excellent ways to foster social development. Even very young children—ages three and up—can benefit from team sports like T-ball and soccer. Team sports provide the opportunity to "naturally" teach children rules, expectations, good sportsmanship and the like. Fun and friendship come along with it too.

I remember watching my son's baseball team in the dugout one day and realizing that those boys were learning to become terrific young men - good citizens - through play and cooperation—no harsh discipline required.

Music, ballet, and the arts are equally valuable in supporting positive social interactions. It is the responsibility of every good parent to provide these enriching avenues for their children.

Chapter 16

Always Hug and Kiss Your Child (Appropriately) and Be Very Welcoming to Their Friends as Well

Growing up with my seven siblings, my parents virtually never hugged us until we were adults—and only after we began hugging them. We became aware through college psychology classes and other relevant books that physical affection, such as hugging, was a significant emotional experience we had been missing. My older sisters and I also began telling our parents that we loved them, as those words had never been spoken in our family. Fortunately, they were able to make some of these changes, which improved our relationship—at least in adulthood.

Our religious background emphasized humility as a key virtue. I don't think we possessed it naturally. During the 1950s and early 1960s, nearly all of my friends were of a similar religion, and I don't believe any of them received praise, hugs, or verbal expressions of love from their parents either. Saying "I love you" to your children simply wasn't done at that time.

It just wasn't done.

The prevailing belief—albeit a false one—was that a parent's primary responsibility was to ensure their child remained humble and never think they were more than they were. As a result, positive interactions that might inflate a child's ego were deliberately avoided. One never wanted to be called a "braggart" or "egotist."

Of course, at the time, this seemed normal. It was rare, if not impossible, to observe other families doing things differently. The cultural norm dictated that children should be raised with strict humility, often at the expense of emotional expression, especially hugging. Some argue that the pendulum has now swung too far in the opposite direction, pointing to permissiveness and exhibited by a trend of awarding every child a trophy. While many experts decry permissiveness, they are inadequate in describing what really works.

But the truth is, handing every child a trophy likely causes little or no harm. Life itself will offer enough adversity as they grow. Parents do not need to create additional adversity; rather, they need to provide a safe environment where problems can be discussed and resolved. A physically distant parent—one who withholds affection such as hugs—creates an atmosphere that lacks emotional safety and comfort.

Children are remarkably intuitive. They can sense when it is emotionally safe to express themselves and work through the adversities that naturally occur in life. For example, a parent cannot control what happens in the classroom or on the playground. A teacher may become a source of stress or fear, and the child's only avenue for processing that experience is through communication with their parents. A third-grader has no other means of problem-solving or expressing their feelings. Without parental support, the child is left alone—alone with fear, anxiety, and uncertainty. In such moments, a hug from a parent can be the most powerful comfort. Without it, the child remains alone, fearful and anxious.

The importance of "contact comfort" was explored in a famous, though controversial, psychology study conducted by American psychologist Harry Harlow. In his experiment, infant rhesus monkeys were presented with two surrogate "mothers": one made of soft cloth and the other made of wire. The wire monkey provided nourishment, while the cloth monkey provided no food—only tactile comfort.

In this study, the experimenter would frighten the monkeys in order to observe their reactions. When scared, the monkeys consistently ran to the cloth mother for comfort and security. Even though the wire mother offered nourishment, it failed to meet the comfort and security needs of the monkeys. The safety, security and comfort of the cloth monkey also enabled the experimental monkeys to explore their environment with greater confidence. In essence, the cloth surrogate signaled to the infant that they were not alone. The monkeys would only visit the wire mother when hungry, returning immediately to the cloth mother for comfort.

Harlow's study (1958) challenged the dominant "learning theory of attachment," which held that infants bonded with caregivers primarily because of nourishment. This study is famous partly because the results were counter to current thinking at the time. Harlow concluded that tactile comfort played a central role in emotional security and attachment, demonstrating that infants have an innate biological need to embrace and cling to a comforting presence—especially when distressed.

We now understand that human babies are much like rhesus monkeys in this regard. While they need nourishment, they will forgo it when emotional safety and comfort are at stake. This finding has profound implications for parenting.

I believe children need "contact comfort" well beyond infancy. While it is critical for bonding in a baby's earliest days, physical affection—hugs, comforting words, and expressions of care—continues to be essential throughout childhood and even into adulthood.

When my son was growing up, he had many friends and they were all welcome in our home. Upon their arrival we consistently hugged them and told them how glad we were to have them over. It seemed to me that many of these children were very happy to receive that hug from both myself and my husband. In addition, breakfast at our house was a common occurrence. During those times, the children (teen boys) would often discuss the problems that were going on in school and sports or any other relevant issue at the time. I believe that our initial "contact comfort" or hugging the boys, both when they arrived and left, at least in part created the safety needed to explore their problems and feelings openly in front of both me and my husband.

If parents fully understood the importance of "contact comfort" from infancy to adulthood and implemented the techniques and principles outlined in this book, they could transform the world—in just one generation.

Chapter 17

Always Listen Carefully to Your Child's Feelings and Help Them Learn and Understand What They Are Feeling

Often, parents do not understand that young children may not know how to label or express their feelings. Most parents don't realize that children must be taught to identify what they're feeling. A toddler may hit, kick, or bite a playmate or sibling as an expression of anger—without fully understanding what they are doing.

One of the most important jobs of a parent is to help children discern what they are feeling and guide them in expressing those feelings in a healthy way.

For example, if your toddler bites a sibling, you might begin by asking why they did it, followed by what they were feeling at the time. A child may explain that they bit their sister because she is mean and they hate her—but the toddler is unaware that their reaction was an expression of anger. It's essential to say, "In this family, we don't bite each other. We use our words and say how we feel" You can then guide the child through the conversation: "You seem mad that she took your toy, and so you bit her, right?" This moment is critical. Then the child can express his feelings right at this time. They can say "I'm mad you took my toy."

When parents avoid this process, children may grow up without being able to understand or articulate their internal experiences, which can lead to poor decision-making and unhealthy relationships. **Feelings are the guideposts to life.** They help us navigate difficult or unfamiliar situations. A child who learns how to identify and express feelings at age two or three will find adult relationships—especially marriage—much easier to navigate. Otherwise, they may end up in marriage counseling learning what could have been taught in toddlerhood.

It's infinitely easier to say, "Go to your room for fighting!" or "I can't stand all this noise—go outside!" than to sit down and walk a child through emotional processing. But avoiding this work can lead to children who are disconnected from their own internal experiences and unable to form happy, functional relationships.

I find it helpful to categorize emotions into four core feelings: **hurt, sad, angry, or afraid**. Countless synonyms fall under these categories. For instance, frustration, aggravation, annoyance, or even rage are all expressions of anger. Rage, however, is often rooted in suppressed emotions from the past. While words like "annoyed" may feel more socially acceptable than saying "angry," the emotion is the same—and it's better if it is labeled accurately.

Labeling feelings is simple in theory but requires a parent's presence and attunement. Children learn to identify emotions when parents listen and help them name what they're feeling. Once a child becomes fluent in labeling emotions, they also need a safe environment—grounded in the parent's calm emotional presence—in which to express them. A child will only express anger, for instance, if they know it is safe to do so. If a parent responds by withdrawing love or punishing the child, the child may begin to suppress emotions or act them out in unhealthy ways. Suppressed anger can lead to depression or chronic anxiety.

Childhood may include many potential traumas: the loss of a pet, the death of a grandparent, or the divorce of parents. These events bring with them the emotion of sadness. While grief encompasses a range of emotions— including anger—the dominant feeling is sadness. Children must be able to process this sadness so it doesn't linger unresolved for a lifetime. Unfortunately, many parents avoid talking about death or divorce, mistakenly thinking it will protect the child. But a functional family includes open discussions about loss and feelings of grief. As a young boy, a client of mine described standing near the open casket of his father and being unable to move any closer. He felt guilty that he felt paralyzed to do so. No one in his family ever discussed the fact that his father died or the impact it had on him and he lived with shame and regret about his inability to be "more of a man." This childhood trauma still affects him today as he felt wrong or bad for what he didn't do even though no one was there to help.

Sometimes a child may seem angry when they're actually hurt or afraid. That's why asking what your child is feeling not only shows that you care, but also helps both of you better understand the situation. If your child becomes withdrawn, you might gently ask, "Are you feeling sad or mad about something? Are you afraid? Hurt?" While you don't want to overwhelm them with questions, careful and compassionate inquiry is key. When my son was about eight or nine years old, I would encourage him to express his feelings as I always had. However, at this age, he wouldn't want to come right out with it in the moment and needed to retreat to his room for extra processing time. At first, I tried to basically pry it out of him until the realization hit me that things had changed and he needed alone time first before he could express how he felt. I couldn't explain why this changed. I needed to accept that my child's way of understanding his feelings at this age was unique and it was important for me to make adjustments.

Many adult emotional issues stem from not learning how to express feelings in childhood. Just as lacking basic math skills would create daily challenges, so too does lacking emotional fluency. Expressing emotions is a learned behavior—and its absence can have serious consequences.

Some parents believe they should always be "respected" and never confronted by their children's emotions—especially anger. This is a false belief, just as it's false to believe that spanking makes children well-behaved (see Chapter One), or that sharing toys is a sign of good character (see Chapter Ten). These beliefs are outdated and often deeply damaging.

According to the *Oxford English Dictionary*, respect is defined as "a feeling of deep admiration for someone or something elicited by their abilities, qualities, or achievements," and as "due regard for the feelings, wishes, rights, or traditions of others." Interestingly, beneath the definition appears the example, *young people's lack of respect for their parents*. That sentence is telling—it reflects how ingrained this issue is in our culture.

There are many who will defend the notion that children must respect their parents—but at what cost?

The danger is that "respect" often becomes a tool for control. True respect is earned. It grows when children feel safe, heard, and valued. If a parent genuinely listens to their child's feelings and helps them resolve emotional challenges, respect will follow naturally. Respect is not an inherited right. It is not automatic simply because you are a parent. Respect for parents by their children must be born out of a sense of love and caring and safety.

There are parents who shame, manipulate, or even physically abuse their children. Do they deserve respect? Are they, by the Oxford definition, giving "due regard" to the child's feelings? If not, it may become impossible for the child to respect them. Fear, not love, becomes the dominant emotional experience. And when fear is present, love cannot exist.

In *Love Is Letting Go of Fear*, Gerald Jampolsky writes that fear and love cannot coexist. If a parent demands "respect" by forbidding emotional expression, the child will experience fear—not love—and certainly not admiration.

They will also experience shame as they are being emotionally abandoned by the parent.

This is the most important reason parents must be attuned to their children's emotions. Without emotional connection, the child internalizes negative messages and concludes that something is wrong with them. This is how the destructive force of **toxic shame** takes root.

In *Healing the Shame That Binds You*, John Bradshaw writes that "toxic shame becomes the core of neurosis, character disorders, political violence, wars, and criminality." He explains, "To have shame as an identity is to believe that one's being is flawed, that one is defective as a human being."

The movie *Good Will Hunting* beautifully illustrates this dynamic. Will, a janitor at MIT, is a mathematical prodigy who solves complex math problems that even the faculty cannot. A professor takes him under his wing, but Will's anger, violence, and emotional detachment stand in the way of his potential. In therapy, it's revealed that Will was brutally abused by his foster father. His therapist finally reaches him by repeating over and over, "It's not your fault. It's not your fault." Will breaks down sobbing—the weight of toxic shame finally beginning to lift. That shame, born of abandonment and abuse, had convinced him that everything was his fault. HIs defenses against his childhood pain included crime, violence and arrogance and an inability to form close lasting relationships.

As parents, we have a profound responsibility to protect our children from toxic shame. Our greatest tool is emotional presence: listening, understanding, and communicating effectively about our children's feelings.

Additionally, children need **mirroring**—a psychological process by which their emotional experiences are acknowledged and reflected back to them. Very young children cannot know who they are without it. Mirroring requires an emotionally available parent. When parents are shut down or disconnected, children are left without reflection, and toxic shame often fills that void. Toxic narcissism is often the result of an early lack of mirroring in the life of an infant.

So how do we help children embrace their emotions?

First, be aware. If your child is angry, sad, afraid, or hurt, name it. If they seem confused, you might say, "It seems like you're mad at Mommy. That's okay. You can tell me." Or if they're sitting alone, ask, "Are you feeling sad about something? Can I help you with what's going on?"

Sit beside them. Get down on their level, eye to eye. Reflect what you see: "You seem mad right now. Can you tell me more about it?"

We are feeling beings. Emotions guide us through life. When children are taught to suppress their feelings, they lose those guideposts—and may spend years trying to find them again.

Suppressed feelings that are not dealt with properly live in the subconscious and shape and effect behavior whether we're aware of them or not. The best way to prevent this is by allowing children to speak about and process their feelings openly. That's how we raise authentic human beings.

When a child says, "I'm hurt because my friend doesn't want to play today," it's not necessary to fix the problem. Feelings don't need to be fixed. They need to be heard. A parent might offer a gentle suggestion: "Why don't you ask your friend to play another day?" But the real power lies in presence and empathy.

The emotional presence of the parent and understanding of the child when they are in some kind of emotional pain is the key here. If trauma occurs, a child who is emotionally supported will not feel alone. We cannot shield our children from all of life's challenges—but we can be there to walk with them through the storm.

Chapter 18

Always Play and Have Fun with Your Child

Because of the nature of the subconscious mind, from birth to early adulthood, parents have the most profound influence children will ever experience. Early learning and interaction create the foundation for who a child will become. With solid parenting, the foundation for a successful and happy life is highly likely. But if early trauma—such as abandonment, violence, or abuse—occurs, children often carry the resulting emotional wounds into adulthood. If not addressed, these subconscious memories can shape relationships and circumstances in ways that seem beyond one's control.

Childhood trauma is the root of many mental health disorders. Even with sustained therapy, adults who were seriously traumatized by their parents may continue to struggle with relationships, work, and daily life.

In *The Myth of Normal*, Gabor Maté describes a traumatic event that occurred when he was fourteen months old. Amid wartime dangers, he was handed over to a "Christian woman to whom my mother entrusted me in the street and who conveyed me to relatives in hiding under relatively safer circumstances." "After being reunited with [my mother]," he writes, "I did not so much as look at her for several days." The trauma left him emotionally detached—a coping mechanism for survival.

Maté argues that it is our *woundedness*, or how we respond to trauma, that dictates much of our adult behavior. He writes, "It can even determine whether or not we are capable of rational thought at all in matters that are of the greatest importance in our lives. For many of us, it rears its head in our closest partnerships, causing all kinds of relational mischief."

Before Freud introduced the unconscious mind to popular awareness, it was commonly believed that children should be "seen and not heard." Parents maintained emotional distance, which was considered both normal and appropriate. The archetypal family of the mid-twentieth century might show a father reading the newspaper in an armchair while the mother cleaned or cooked and the children played unsupervised. The father often remained detached, with the mother intervening only to discipline or direct. British television and film have frequently portrayed this model. Boarding school, even for children as young as eight, has long been considered both respectable and desirable in certain cultures.

Before the unconscious mind was widely understood, children were believed to simply "grow up" on their own. It was not commonly accepted that parenting profoundly shaped emotional development.

Fortunately, we now have extensive research on the psychology of early childhood and the power of the subconscious. We know that children long for their parents' attention and unconditional love. Their survival depends on this attachment, and they will do nearly anything to preserve it—even if it means suppressing their own feelings and instincts. This comes at a cost: they may compromise their authenticity to maintain the bond.

As parents, we must recognize our enormous influence, our unbounded power—and the responsibility that comes with it. That power can easily be abused by parents who are uninformed or who seek control rather than connection. Children, with limited defenses, may become hypervigilant—scanning for changes in a parent's emotional state in order to protect themselves from unpredictable moods or reactions.

I offer this context to emphasize just how important it is to **play** with your children. Play creates a solid foundation between parent and child which can be relied upon during more difficult times.

Play is the work of young children (see Chapter Six), and when parents join in, the benefits multiply. Play provides countless teaching opportunities and builds a foundation of security, love, and connection. When parents play with their children, they are sending a powerful message: *"What you do is important, and I want to be a part of it."*

Having fun is essential to childhood. Parents are often preoccupied with milestones—reading, math, test scores. I say those things will come. What matters most is joy. Have as much fun with your child as you possibly can, within your individual circumstances. The benefits far outweigh those of any structured activity.

Read together. Watch movies. Play board games. Do puzzles. Toss a football or a baseball. Build sandcastles. Attend a concert or a play. Visit a zoo or a museum. Go to a theme park. Laugh, explore, ride bikes, jump rope—*just play*. You have your children for an incredibly short period of time. These experiences bring joy, emotional stability, and a deep sense of safety to your child's world.

Fun is also the easiest and most natural way to teach relationship skills, love, cooperation, and joy. It doesn't take much effort. In fact, it can teach almost anything. Ride bikes and talk about safety and balance. Point out flowers, trees, and buildings. Or just laugh and be silly. That shared joy is transformative.

Children will almost always say yes when invited to have fun. There are no rules—just connection. Silliness and spontaneity work like magic to create a lasting emotional bond. It's simple. It's powerful. **Practice it.**

Having fun together builds a foundation of emotional closeness that will sustain your relationship during difficult times. If you lose your job, become ill, or suffer a personal loss, your children will be more likely to stay close and offer support—because you've been there for them. But if parenting has been marked by harsh discipline or emotional distance, children will likely withdraw in your time of need. If your usual emotional state turns even darker due to adversity, they may flee for protection rather than run to comfort you.

There is so much to be gained from having fun with your children. It is one of the simplest, most effective tools we have to nurture emotional health, build lasting bonds, and prepare our children—and ourselves—for life's inevitable challenges.

Chapter 19

Always let your child make choices

Developmental Psychologist Erik Erikson developed eight psychosocial stages of development, beginning at birth and continuing through death. His second stage, **Autonomy vs. Shame and Doubt**, encompasses the toddler years, roughly from 18 months to three years of age. However, I believe that the learning of autonomy continues throughout childhood and into young adulthood.

Erikson proposed that each psychosocial stage presents a unique developmental challenge. A child will either successfully achieve a positive psychological quality or fail to develop it. Each stage offers an opportunity for personal growth—but also carries the risk of failure. In the second stage, Erikson emphasized the development of personal control. As toddlers naturally begin to assert some independence, this stage presents an ideal window to help children learn how to make choices and gain confidence. Ideally, children should emerge with a sense of autonomy, not with feelings of shame or self-doubt.

One of the most significant tasks during this stage is potty training. It is critical that children are *not* shamed or punished for accidents or mistakes. Only consistent, positive encouragement allows them to find success and develop confidence in mastering this milestone.

Although toilet training is central to this developmental phase, there are many other opportunities for children to build autonomy. One of the most effective tools is allowing them to make small daily choices. This strategy can also help reduce the conflict that often arises with independent-minded toddlers. If a child is constantly told what to do, frustration may build—and with it, behavioral challenges.

For example, let's say you want your child to clean up their toys. Instead of commanding, "Put your toys away now!" you might say:

"Johnny, Mommy would like you to put away your toys. You can do it now or in ten minutes. But if the toys aren't picked up after ten minutes, we'll have to delay going outside to play. It's your choice—what would you like to do?"

If Johnny chooses to wait ten minutes, you can respond, *"Okay, I'm glad you're making this choice for yourself."* Ideally, he will follow through. However, it's likely he may test your resolve. If he doesn't clean up, the consequence—delayed playtime—must be enforced. Whether or not he picks up the toys is less important than the lesson: choices carry consequences.

The key takeaways:

1. Teach your child to make choices by presenting options.

2. Allow the child to experience the natural consequences of those choices.

This approach is far more effective than the parent acting as a constant enforcer of negative consequences. It also nurtures intrinsic motivation, rather than relying on external authority to drive positive behavior. When children are given age-appropriate choices, they develop personal control, confidence, decision-making skills, and a deeper sense of security.

Of course, the choices you offer must be within reason and developmentally appropriate. You wouldn't ask a three-year-old whether they want to cross a busy street or let them use a sharp knife to butter their bread. Common sense must prevail.

That said, allowing a child to choose their clothing is a safe and empowering choice—*if* they are interested. There is no need to force decision-making if a child isn't inclined. But if they are, present a few appropriate options.

When my son was two years old, he adored *101 Dalmatians*. He had Dalmatian sheets, pillows, and a special "puppy shirt," which he insisted on wearing nearly every day until he outgrew it. It received more washings than I can count. Still, it was his choice—and honoring that choice strengthened our bond. Insisting that he vary his wardrobe would have served no constructive purpose.

Food choices can be trickier. You might offer an apple or an orange, but we all know it's rarely that simple. Still, if your home contains only the foods you want your child to eat, those will be their available choices. If your child eats pizza or fries at a neighbor's house and these are not your approved choices, you can simply say, *"In this house, we eat foods we believe are good for us. Other families may make different choices, and that's okay."*

Occasional deviations from your regimen won't harm your child. In fact, they provide a healthy opportunity to learn that different people make different choices. Judgment isn't required—only understanding. You may not allow sweet foods in your home. Yet, at a birthday party, let them eat cake and the ice cream!

One of the most helpful phrases I learned as a parent is: *"In this house, we…"*

For instance, when your child asks why their friend gets to stay up until 11 p.m. watching cartoons, you can calmly reply, *"In this house, we believe it's best to go to bed at 9 p.m."* This approach avoids criticism of others while reinforcing your family's values and structure. It reinforces a child's sense of belonging to something unique—a family culture, a tribe. That sense of belonging enhances trust and emotional security.

I cannot overstate the importance of this principle. When children are offered meaningful choices, they learn decision-making—a critical adult skill. I grew up in a large family of eight children. Resources were limited, and my father was the unquestioned authority. We mostly functioned as a group, and in this tribe we had few opportunities to make individual choices. As an adult, I realized that decision-making didn't come naturally to me; I had had little practice. Over time I learned, but I often wondered why others seemed to make decisions with such ease, while I struggled with doubt and second-guessing.

Your child will also make mistakes. But it's better to make small missteps under a parent's protection than to enter adulthood without the tools to make decisions confidently. With thoughtful guidance, your child can develop autonomy and self-trust—skills that will serve them for life.

Chapter 20

Always Look Within Yourself to Assess Your Parenting Motives and Behaviors

Although this is the last rule in my book, it may be the most important one.

Certain skills can be taught, and in learning these skills, you automatically become a better parent. For example, in understanding Rule #7, you've decided not to call your child names. This may include holding yourself back when you're tempted to tell your child they are lazy, ungrateful, or use any other negative descriptor. If you're remembering Rule #7, you won't let yourself proceed down this most destructive road.

But if a name comes flying out of your mouth when your child doesn't clean their room after you've asked nicely, it's most likely because you were called that name—or something similar—when you were a child. The unconscious mind can override our conscious thinking, decisions, and actions. If there are unconscious motives that have not been examined or healed, they may control you unless you bring them into full awareness.

You may have the best intentions to be fully aware of how you're treating your children, yet still find yourself unable to follow through—because of past pain, hurt, or trauma that remains unprocessed or unresolved.

If you were called names that are buried deep in your memory—especially if those names were deeply painful to hear—you may find it difficult to stop yourself from repeating them when your child acts in a certain way. You may even justify the name-calling, believing the child "deserved it." If one of your parents repeatedly told you that you were lazy, and you believed it at the time, you may observe your child acting in a way that triggers that memory. You may think: *Well, he is being lazy,* because the false belief is still embedded in your psyche. That belief must be brought into conscious awareness in order to be changed.

Children Are Not Lazy

Children are not lazy. Children are energetic, curious, and eager learners—if given the proper environment, freedom, and love. They may even comply with your requests if they are free of underlying anger or hurt that may be blocking their cooperation.

Any childhood trauma you experienced can affect your parenting. You may have been emotionally isolated—and still feel that isolation today. If you are unaware of the pain caused by your parents' inability to meet your emotional needs, then it is likely you will unintentionally repeat the same behavior with your children. Often, this happens without conscious awareness.

The subconscious is powerful and can drive behavior in destructive ways. For example, if you were frequently physically left alone, you may view that abandonment as "normal" and, in turn, leave your children alone too often. The subconscious employs defense mechanisms to keep painful memories out of our awareness—we don't want to remember or feel the pain of having been left alone too often or too long, in essence being abandoned.

Children do not want to blame their parents for their shortcomings. Instead, they blame themselves. This is the origin of **toxic shame**.

A child who is emotionally abandoned may think that, if they could just say or do the right thing, their parents would change—and finally understand what the child needs.

Because survival (both emotional and physical) is paramount, a child must blame themselves for their parents' shortcomings. The fear of losing a parent's love is too great. The child must choose between *attachment* (staying in good graces with the parent) and *authenticity* (being true to oneself).

Children may come to believe that they are somehow fundamentally flawed, wrong, or defective when their needs aren't properly met. This is a survival mechanism, and for children, it is often highly effective. The problems begin in adulthood, when those children attempt to form functional relationships with friends or partners—only then does the failure of this system reveal itself.

There is a saying: *What protected us as children often destroys us as adults.*

The abandonment children experience nearly always results in toxic shame. Again, this shame arises because the child cannot afford to blame their "survival figure." Instead, the child assumes: *Everything that's wrong is my fault.* Attachment is life-sustaining and cannot be threatened. To maintain that attachment, children will often suppress who they are and how they feel. If a parent refuses to allow the child to express anger, the child will suppress their authenticity to preserve the relationship.

That anger will likely be internalized, possibly turn into depression, or be acted out in unrelated situations.

Defense Mechanisms and the Subconscious

In order to survive and cope with emotional experiences, the subconscious mind creates defense mechanisms. These are strategies used to protect oneself from anxiety, stress, or uncomfortable emotions—often by distorting reality.

Most defense mechanisms are rooted in the psychoanalytic theory of Sigmund Freud. Some examples include:

- **Repression** – Unconsciously blocking painful thoughts or feelings from awareness (e.g., forgetting a traumatic event).

- **Denial** – Refusing to see or admit a painful truth (e.g., the first stage of grief).

- **Projection** – Attributing your own unacceptable feelings or thoughts to someone else.

- **Displacement** – Redirecting your emotions to a more acceptable or vulnerable target (e.g., kicking the dog after a bad day at work).

- **Sublimation** – Channeling unacceptable feelings like anger into productive outlets (e.g., sports or creative work).

- **Regression** – Reverting to childlike behavior in response to stress (e.g., becoming irrational and throwing a tantrum).

- **Rationalization** – Offering self-justifying explanations for unpleasant behaviors ("I didn't want to win anyway").

- **Dissociation** – Emotionally detaching from reality to avoid painful feelings.

Additional mechanisms include intellectualization, reaction formation, suppression, compartmentalization, undoing, splitting, identification, introjection, compensation, humor, altruism, fantasy, acting out, passive aggression, idealization, devaluation, and avoidance.

Some of these mechanisms—like sublimation and humor—can be adaptive. However, they all serve the same fundamental purpose: to protect us from anxiety, stress, or emotional pain. Any coping mechanism developed to survive childhood trauma can be classified under one or more of these defense strategies.

Their complexity and variety illustrate the unconscious mind's immense power to shield us from pain. Most of these strategies are formed in childhood and carried into adulthood, where they often hinder the development of healthy, functional relationships.

This underscores the importance of healing childhood wounds. Adults—especially those raising children—must bring their unconscious pain into awareness to avoid passing it on to their vulnerable children.

When Pain Is Passed Down

Some of my clients have experienced the transmission of violent or destructive unconscious motives from their parents to themselves.

One female client experienced severe punishment as a four-year-old. If she displeased her father, he would remove his belt, make her pull down her pants to expose bare skin, and lash her multiple times. During these beatings, he would say, "This hurts me more than it hurts you." She had to kneel beside her bed for support, trying not to fall forward with each lashing.

Her father lacked control over his violence and held the delusional belief that he was "disciplining" her for her own good. He was most likely engaging in denial—or possibly dissociation—to avoid acknowledging the horrific nature of his actions.

Another male client currently struggles with money management. His father abandoned the family when he was a child. Though his mother was a capable realtor and supported the family for about six months, she eventually left her job to take a minimum-wage position. Her intent–though irrational–for the low wage job was to punish her ex-husband. That desire prevailed over caring for her children. As a result, the family lived in poverty. Her decision was an expression of unprocessed anger—likely made without conscious awareness of the harm it caused her children.

I've even read tragic news stories of fathers dropping children off bridges in attempts to punish the mother. The consequences of unexamined emotional pain can be extreme and deadly.

Self-Knowledge Is a Parenting Prerequisite

Our suppressed unconscious feelings can lead to outrageous consequences—including death—when they are buried or acted on impulsively in the belief that doing so will relieve the pain. We cannot overstate the importance of self-awareness in parenting. Raising emotionally healthy children requires profound self-understanding.

Before the influence of thinkers like Sigmund Freud, most people lacked insight into the psychological effects parenting had on children. Many believed that personality was fixed at birth, and they failed to recognize the consequences of abusive or negligent parenting.

Thankfully, today we are more informed. We understand the importance of emotional intelligence—for ourselves and our children. We now recognize that corporal punishment, such as beating a child with a belt, is violence and abuse.

We also know that how we treat our children determines whether cycles of generational dysfunction continue—or end.

When we choose to educate ourselves and do the inner work required to raise emotionally healthy children, we hold the power to change the world—in just one generation.

Bibliography

American Academy of Pediatrics. *Policy Statement.* 2018.

Bos, Bev. *Together We're Better: Establishing Coactive Environments for Young Children.* Turn the Page Press, 1990.

Bradshaw, John. *Healing the Shame That Binds You.* Revised ed., Health Communications, Inc., 1993.

Cherry, Kendra MSEd. "Erikson's Stages of Development: A Closer Look at the Eight Psychosocial Stages." *Verywell Mind*, August 3, 2022. www.verywellmind.com.

Cole-Whittaker, Terry. *How to Have More in a Have-Not World.* Fawcett Crest, 1983.

Durrant, Joan, and Ron Ensom. "Physical Punishment of Children: Lessons from 20 Years of Research." *CMAJ* 184, no. 12 (2012): 1373–77.

Freud, Sigmund. *Introductory Lectures on Psychoanalysis.* New York: Liveright, 1920.

Gayle, Nirvana Reginald. "The Truth About Spare the Rod and Spoil the Child." *Patheos*, November 2014. www.patheos.com.

Ginott, Haim G. *Teacher and Child: A Book for Parents and Teachers.* Macmillan, 1972.

Goleman, Daniel. *Emotional Intelligence: Why It Can Matter More than IQ.* Bantam Books, 1995.

Harlow, Harry F. "The Nature of Love." *American Psychologist* 13, no. 12 (1958): 673–85. https://doi.org/10.1037/h0047884.

HBR's 10 Must Reads on Emotional Intelligence. Harvard Business Review, 2015.

Isaacson, Walter. *Elon Musk.* Simon & Schuster, 2023.

Jampolsky, Gerald G. *Love Is Letting Go of Fear.* 3rd ed., Celestial Arts, 2010.

Jung, Carl G. *The Archetypes and the Collective Unconscious.* Translated by R. F. C. Hull. 2nd ed. Vol. 9, Part 1 of *The Collected Works of C. G. Jung.* Princeton University Press, 1968.

Kohn, Alfie. *Punished by Rewards.* Houghton Mifflin, 1993.

Maté, Gabor. *The Myth of Normal.* Avery, 2022.

Rosenthal, Robert, and Lenore Jacobson. *Pygmalion in the Classroom: Teacher Expectation and Pupils' Intellectual Development.* Holt, Rinehart and Winston, 1968.

Skinner, B. F. *Beyond Freedom and Dignity.* New York: Knopf, 1974.

Zukav, Gary. *The Heart of the Soul.* Simon & Schuster, 2001.

About the Author

Susan M. Thomson, PhD, is a Master Certified Addictions Counselor and Life Coach. In 1985, she graduated from Tulane University in New Orleans, Louisiana, with a degree in experimental social psychology.

Before earning her doctorate, she taught special needs children, including those with severe learning disabilities and developmental delays who had been mainstreamed into regular classrooms. While teaching, she worked closely with school psychologists and speech pathologists to address the needs of individual students. She also taught psychology courses at the junior college level. From 1988 to 1993, as a Licensed Professional Counselor, she owned and operated her own eating disorders clinic, providing both individual and group therapy.

In 1993, following the birth of her son, she relocated to La Jolla, California. At that time, she turned her focus to parenting and volunteer work in local schools. She became president of the board at The Children's School, where her son was a student. Alongside her husband, Darryl Tschirn, she established the Tschirn Family Library, which remains in place today. In collaboration with other parents, she co-founded a charter school—Explorer Elementary—emphasizing a social-emotional learning curriculum. She also served as president of its board.

Later, she became president of the Parents' Association at The Bishop's School (grades 6–12), meeting weekly with the headmaster and leading monthly association meetings.

While living in La Jolla, she was appointed vice chair of the Human Relations Commission, an advisory body to the Office of the Mayor of San Diego. In 2015, she received a Certificate of Congressional Recognition from U.S. Congressman Scott Peters for her work in the fight against human trafficking. The San Diego Human Relations Commission also honored her with a Special Commendation for her efforts in human trafficking prevention and restorative justice.

In addition, she served four years as vice president of the La Jolla Shores Association, where she received a Special Commendation for Leadership from San Diego City Council President Pro Tem Barbara Bry.

Susan M. Thomson, PhD
Services

Dr. Susan M. Thomson is available for speaking engagements, life coaching, parenting counseling, and addiction counseling. Susan can be reached at: **858-531-5346** or **Tmephd@aol.com**.

For more information, visit her website: https://www.ParentingTheRules.com

You can access her website via this QR code.

Parenting: The Rules

International Best Seller Status

www.ingramcontent.com/pod-product-compliance
Lightning Source LLC
Chambersburg PA
CBHW051529120626
46551CB00012B/1149